JOHN S. MBITI is Africa's best-known Christian theologian. He has taught in several African universities and at Union Theological Seminary in New York City. Professor Mbiti is currently Director of the Ecumenical Institute of the World Council of Churches in Geneva. He is the author of *Concepts of God in Africa*, *African Religions and Philosophy*, *New Testament Eschatology in an African Background*, *Love and Marriage in Africa*, and *Akamba Stories*.

The Prayers of African Religion

The Prayers of African Religion

JOHN S. MBITI

ORBIS BOOKS

Maryknoll, New York 10545

Library of Congress Cataloging in Publication Data

Mbiti, John S
  The prayers of African religion.

  1. Prayers.   2. African—Religion.   I. Title.
BV245.M484   1976   299'.6   75-42519
ISBN 0-88344-394-5

First published 1975 by SPCK, London
Copyright © 1975 John S. Mbiti
Manufactured in the United States of America

For our children
Kyeni, Maria, and Esther
in their endeavours to
communicate with
the Eternal

Contents

Preface

I wish to record my gratitude to the Reverend Clement Janda for assisting me in collecting many of the prayers included in this book. At the time, he was my student in the Department of Religious Studies and Philosophy, Makerere University, Uganda. I am also grateful to my secretary in the same department, Miss Josephine Ssali, for typing most of the manuscript.

There are slightly over 300 prayers included in this book, although the numbering goes up to only 288. This is because some prayers are grouped under one number (e.g., 87, 147, 182, and so on) if they happen to belong to one occasion or if they make better sense when put together like that. The numbering is given only for the purpose of making easy reference to the prayers. The grouping of the prayers into chapters is also to facilitate the use of the book, and to demonstrate the wide variety of prayers that exists even when they are offered for the same purpose. No doubt many of them can be put under two or more chapter groupings. The commentaries to the prayers are no more than introductory remarks to open the way for deeper understanding and appreciation of the prayers. It is impossible, however, to give here a background to the African peoples who have formulated these prayers. Such a background would put them in their proper setting in life (*Sitz im Leben*, as it were), but though extremely valuable, it would take up a lot of space and perhaps make the book rather cumbersome. The names of African peoples from which the prayers come are indicated in the notes, together with their countries, as well as the sources of the prayers and sometimes brief explanations.

The number of African prayers must range in the thousands. But, alas, most of them are not yet recorded in writing. What I have included here are the ones to which I had access through written sources. This was the only practicable way to consider a large part of the continent, since it was impossible to make the collection through direct field-work. The selection of prayers included here contains practically all the written material that I could find, omitting only a few prayers which would have made no appreciable difference to the content of the book or the analysis of the material.

The sources from which I have taken the prayers are, therefore, mainly secondary and some are at third hand. As such they have their own limitations and their reliability is not the same throughout. I was fully aware of these limitations in making this collection; but the prayers, even as they appear here, have their academic usefulness which should not be overlooked. One quarter of the sources of the material are African scholars and students, while the rest are (or were) foreigners—mainly missionaries, anthropologists, research students and administrators. Although the sources come from the period between 1895 and 1974, the majority of the prayers date much earlier, thus being very close to, and in some cases exactly, what they were in pre-colonial days and before the penetration of Christianity into the interior of Africa. In some cases the sources give the prayers in their original African languages, but here I have used only the English translations as provided by the authors of the material (unless otherwise indicated in the notes). In spite of the limitations of these sources, and the small number of prayers accessible to me, this book is put out as a small contribution towards a better understanding of African religion in particular and the religions of mankind in general.

I am grateful to the publishers for their co-operation and encouragement in the production of the book.

JOHN MBITI

Acknowledgements

Thanks are due to the following for permission to quote from copyright sources:

J. J. Augustin, Inc., Publisher, Locust Valley, New York: *Dahomey*, vol. I, by M. J. Herskovits

Cambridge University Press: *The Anatomy of Lango Religion*, by T. T. S. Hayley; *The Bakitara or Banyoro*, by J. Roscoe

Frank Cass & Co. Ltd: *With a Prehistoric People*, by W. S. and K. Routledge

Rosica Colin Ltd: *The Prayers of Man*, ed. by A. M. di Nola

Finnish Society for Missiology and Ecumenics, Helsinki: *God and the Sun in Meru Thought*, by R. Harjula

Ghana High Commission: *Akim-Kotoku, an Oman of the Gold Coast*, by J. M. Field

International African Institute: *The Ngoni of Nyasaland*, by M. Read; *Reaction to Conquest*, by M. Wilson Hunter

Longman Group Ltd and Praeger Publishers, Inc.: *Olodumare: God in Yoruba Belief*, by E. B. Idowu

Macmillan London and Basingstoke: *The Ila Speaking Peoples of Northern Rhodesia*, by E. W. Smith and A. M. Dale; *Religion of the Hottentots and Bushmen*, by A. de Quatrefages

Makerere University Press, Kampala: 'Funeral rites and ceremonies of remembering the Departed among the Basoga', Occasional Research Paper No. 148, by J. L. Mbotana

William Morrow & Co., Inc., New York: *The Masai, Herders of East Africa*, by S. Bleeker

Oxford University Press: *Akiga's Story*, by R. East; *The Bantu of Northern Kavirondo*, vol. II, by G. Wagner; *Conversations with Ogotemmeli: an Introduction to Dogon Religious Ideas*, by M. Griaule; *Divinity and Experience: the Religion of the Dinka*, by G. Lienhardt; *Karimojong Politics*, by N. Dyson Hudson; *The Masai*, by A. C. Hollis; *The Nandi*, by A. C. Hollis; *Nuer Religion*, by E. E. Evans-Pritchard; *The Position of the Chief in the Modern Political System of Ashanti*, by K. A. Busia; *Religion and Art in Ashanti*, by R. S. Rattray; *Religion and Medicine of the Ga People*, by J. M. Field; *The Suk, their Language and Folklore*, by M. W. H. Beech; *Witchcraft, Oracles and Magic among the Azande*, by E. E. Evans-Pritchard

Pastoral Institute, Kampala: *The Word That Lives*, by A. Shorter

Routledge & Kegan Paul: *People of the Small Arrow*, by J. H. Driberg; (and Praeger Publishers, Inc.) *Child of Two Worlds*, by G. M. Gatheru; (and

Humanities Press) *Pagan Tribes of the Nilotic Sudan*, by C. G. and B. Z. Seilgman; (and Humanities Press) *The Social Institutions of the Kipsigis*, by J. G. Peristiany

Seeley, Service & Co. Ltd: *Among the Bantu Nomads*, by J. T. Brown; *In the Heart of Bantu Land*, by D. Campbell; *In Witchbound Africa*, by F. H. Melland

Tavistock Publications Ltd: *Man in Africa*, edited by M. Douglas and P. M. Kaberry

H. F. & G. Witherby Ltd: *West African Secret Societies*, by F. W. Butt-Thompson

Thanks are also due to National Arts of Tanzania Ltd for permission to use a photograph of a Makonde carving by Sita as a basis for the cover design.

1 *Introduction*

AFRICA'S SPIRITUAL RICHES

Praying forms an integral part of any viable religious system. African religion is rich in prayers. Hitherto these prayers have never been collected from the different African societies who have created them and integrated them into their religious life. This volume of 300 African prayers contains only a small portion of the many thousands of such prayers which no doubt exist, most of them having been handed down through the generations. Others continue to be created as the occasions arise and demand. This collection is a clear demonstration of Africa's spiritual riches. The prayers, more than any other aspect of religion, contain the most intense expression of African traditional spirituality. A study of these prayers takes us to the core of African spirituality, and adds a valuable dimension to our understanding of African religion.

Studies of African religion have generally included something on prayers, and in some cases a few prayers. But a study of the prayers by themselves in any considerable length has long been overdue. These prayers contain insight into many aspects of religious and philosophical thought of African peoples, such as the concepts of God, man, the world, spirits, good and evil, etc. The prayers show us both the depths of soul-searching and the heights of spiritual venture, in a way not possible through other religious exercises and beliefs.

The praying tradition is well established in African societies. But we do not have enough knowledge about this tradition to understand how it developed historically through the generations. Most of the prayers have literary forms which clearly indicate that they have been used repeatedly and may have originated several generations ago. Other prayers do not seem to have enjoyed long or wide usage, as they were created for given occasions. Their usage was consequently limited. The themes covered in these prayers are almost timeless, at least as far as Africans are concerned, and it would be reasonable, therefore, to guess that people have for dozens of centuries prayed for the same things. These would include, for example, prayers for recovery from illness, protection against danger, for prosperity and success, offspring, rain, and so on. The exact wording has changed from time to time, but the needs which have occasioned the prayers, as well as the contents of most of these prayers, have not changed considerably through the centuries.

We may assume that praying has always been the core of African religion, and some of the prayer formulas we have here may have originated from the earliest beginnings of African religion. May it not be possible, too, that praying was the original element of religious consciousness called for by the difficult circumstances in which early man found himself and for which he had to solicit help from someone other than his fellow human beings? We make no claims to resolve the complex question of the origin of praying. But many of the prayers in this book clearly show that they are concerned with African issues of human life which have not become radically different from what they might have been five to ten thousand years ago. Therefore, praying would seem to be one of the most ancient items of African spiritual riches.

WHO PRAYS AND TO WHOM

Most of these prayers are recited by people in their official capacities as priests, diviners, medicine-men, kings, ritual and family elders, and heads of family or other social groups (e.g. hunters). Consequently, such prayers are said on behalf of the group or community concerned, or on behalf of individuals belonging to the group. Comparatively few prayers are uttered by individuals for their personal or private needs, e.g. for prosperity (56), for a family spirit (75), divination before going to hunt alone (85). Thus, as a rule, these African prayers are community-based and community-orientated. Many of those which begin with or include personal requests are orientated towards the needs of other people.

A good number of the prayers are set in a responsive form which emphasizes the group or community participation in prayer and shows also that the concerns expressed in the prayers are common or shared concerns. The leader may intone the prayer while the assembled group responds in song or recitation, generally repeating some of the phrases uttered by the leader, or a well-known formula. Examples can be seen in prayers 14, 31, 40, 41, 47, 48, 57 and 59.

We may say that everyone prays even when only official leaders may be reciting the words. Everyone prays in the sense that all those present are party to the contents of the prayers, and sometimes participate by repeating some of the words of the leader or a given formula. Those who are in need are free to pray or present their needs to the officiating leaders or to have other people pray on their behalf. Therefore we have, for example, prayers of the king for his country and subjects (17–20), of parents for their children and relatives (33, 34, 39, 47), of friends for a woman having a difficult delivery (126), the medicine-man in his work (77–81), the wife for her husband who is at war (104), a dying man (140), the cultivators as they go about their work of sowing, weeding, and harvesting (66–75), and so on. We do not, however, have prayers specifically uttered by children: instead, they join their communities when they assemble for prayer at home or elsewhere. Generally the older members of the family pray on behalf of everyone, or else the local ritual or prayer leaders say these prayers for everyone else. Both women and men say the prayers and there is no sex discrimination.

The addressees of the prayers are numerous. Most of the prayers are addressed directly and specifically to God. He is, normally, mentioned by his personal or attributive name but sometimes he is addressed only by implication. We shall see in the next section something of the portrait of God which emerges in these prayers. He is the prime addressee, and we need not point out which prayers support this statement since this is obvious and applies to at least nine out of ten prayers.

A few, not more than ten per cent, are addressed to divinities, spirits, the living dead, and personifications of nature (trees, rivers, earth, etc.). Examples of these are 14 (second part), 15, 16, 18, 20 and many of the prayers in ch. 8. In a very few cases we have prayers addressed to national heroes and founders, or which make reference to them while addressing God. We cite three examples of these: prayers 31, 275 and 276 mention Kunda (the clan founder of the Ngombe), 59 mentions Lenana (a Masai hero), 215 and 230 mention Nyikang (the national founder or hero of the Shilluk).

The prayers are addressed to the spiritual realities, of which African peoples are very much aware. These realities include God, who is supreme over all, various types of spirits, personifications of natural phenomena and objects, some of which (like the sun) are regarded as manifestations of God. God is not always distinguished clearly from the other spiritual realities; in some prayers the address may simply be directed to them all collectively, or just to the world of spiritual realities regardless of who may pay attention to it 'there'.

SPIRITUAL REALITIES

We can look at these realities in some detail as they are revealed in the prayers.

God: At least 90 per cent of the prayers are addressed to God. Therefore he emerges as the clearest and most concrete spiritual reality. A great deal is said about him and we can only list some of the outstanding points. The picture of God which emerges from these prayers is consistent with African ideas of God elsewhere in the increasingly large literature already available, but our discussion will confine itself to the contents of the prayers in this volume.

God is approached first and foremost as Father and Creator (Maker, Fashioner, Originator, Source). There are innumerable prayers which address him specifically as Father and/or Creator. Even where no use of either 'father' or 'creator' is made, many prayers imply that they are uttered to God who has made people and who cares for them, loves them and listens to them as their Father. The hungry man prays for food, prosperity, and children to God 'my Father' (7); and at evening one turns in prayer to the Father who will help (10). People invoke him as 'our (my) Father' (21, 113, 124, 227, 240, 257), 'Father of (our, the) fathers' (21, 257), 'Father God' (28), 'Father' (63, 133, 140, 179, 239), 'the Father' (174), 'Father of our race' (133), 'Father who never dies' (133). Therefore people have a feeling of confidence towards God since he is their Father. They have access to him, they appeal to him freely, and look up to him to look after them. God is also called upon as 'our Grandfather' (60), 'great Elder' (259), and 'Mother' (female 139, 225). The attribute of the fatherhood or motherhood of God serves to put him in a family relationship with people: he is their origin, their parent, their protector, their provider, their shelter. Consequently they pose and speak of themselves as God's children.

Frequently God is addressed as Creator (or Maker), an attribute which is very closely related to that of being Father. He is invoked as 'Creator of everything and omniscient' (28), to whom offerings and prayers are made (226, etc.), to whom people dedicate their seeds at sowing time (66) since he makes the seeds germinate and sprout (67). People turn to him at the time of starvation, to deliver them from death, 'for thou art our Father and we are thy children. Thou hast created us . . .' (113). When people are concerned over barrenness, they appeal to him so that he may create life (babies) in the barren women because 'Thou . . . art our Father and hast created all of us' (124). A dying man calls upon him as his Creator to help him (140), while the parents of a newly born baby offer it as a 'fresh bud' to 'the Creator. . . the Powerful' (199).

Thus human life begins from God, continues in God and ends with God. As the Creator of all things, people acknowledge him to be the only One who 'alone hast created us' (243). He is both far ('up there') and 'near', and invisible (245). A psalm of creation reminds people that God created all things like the sun, the moon and the stars which are 'born and die and come again', as well as man who 'is born and dies and comes not again' (244). As Creator he is the Fountain of life: 'The Source of being is above, which gives life to men. . . . That they may live prosperously' (248). Prayer 252 is in praise of God as Creator who piles up 'the rocks into towering mountains', makes rain so that rivers flow, sews 'the heavens like cloth', 'bringest forth the shoots that they stand erect', and fills 'the land with mankind'. Though God has created every-thing, people feel grateful, nevertheless, and when he gives them babies some of them pause to thank him as conferring on them a great worth (262). As Creator, God is asked in innumerable prayers to give people offspring, wealth and health. He is referred to in one prayer (63) as 'Husband of the cows, Husband of the women' by which it is meant that he creates ('husbands') new life in all living things.

God is regarded and called upon as 'the Protector who looks after the country' (214), to whom appeal is made for protection in time of war, adversity or other danger (ch. 6). As Creator, God listens to, and hears, people appealing to him (213, 276, 277). Indeed, praying to God assumes that he listens to people and pays attention to their communication. He is 'our Refuge' (255) in all conditions and eventualities of life.

God is praiseworthy and thankworthy. This comes out in a number of prayers. He is praised as the 'Seven Heavens, Seven Earths' (238), 'the Great Man' (239), 'Great Spirit' (252), 'the Great God' (253). Therefore people 'praise Thee, Thou that art God' (256, 254, see also chapter 12). He is so thankworthy, that one finds 'no words to thank you' (259), and the birth of a child is one of the many occasions when he is thanked. Yet in African life thanks are expressed more in deeds than in words, and for that reason we do not find frequent use of words like 'thank' or 'thanksgiving' in these prayers. When people sacrifice or make offerings to God, these acts serve, among other things, to express people's gratitude to him, especially at harvest time (70, 71), at the end of a successful hunting expedition (87), or in connection with the healing of the sick (49, 227). Other praise names for God include: 'Morning Star that rises forth' and 'God to whom prayer is made' (222), 'the Maker of the stars and the Pleiades' (253), Bilikonda ('the unendingness of the forest, the Eternal, the everlasting One', 276), the 'Wonderful One' (252), 'the Great Mantle which covers us' (253), the 'Gracious One' (252), 'the King and Ruler of all things' (227, 259, 277), and so on.

God is invisible, without ending (276), eternal (247), the Ancient, 'In the beginning was God' (247, 213), 'the great Elder' (259), omnipresent', 'in the heavens and below' (28), holy (cf. 168, 238), and Almighty (23, 66, 77, 105, 128, 199). God is omniscient (28): 'Thou hast two eyes that see well both by day and by night' (265). He is immortal: 'In the beginning was God, Today is God, Tomorrow will be God' (247), 'Thou who art deathless, Who knowest not death, Who livest always' (133). God is utterly other: 'Nzame [God] is Nzame, Man is Man: Each to himself, each in his dwelling' (242), 'Today we, your creatures, prostrate ourselves before you in supplication. We have no strength. You who have created us have all power' (66). He cannot be depicted in pictorial forms: 'Who can make an image of God? He has no body. He is as a word which comes out of your mouth . . . ' (247). He is transcendent and most high (230), dwelling on high (242, 252), 'the Man on High' (172, 229) to whom people 'cry out for rain' (172, cf. 170).

God is the 'great Spirit' who is continually active in creating (252), and who 'is as a word which comes out of your mouth. That word! It is no more, It is past, and still it lives!' (247). The medicine-man addresses him as the 'Spirit of virile energy . . . Spirit of Force' (77). People summon one another to pray to him, for: 'The Spirit of the Air is something great, Pursuing us over his wide plains' (231). He loves man (247), and people would argue that if God did not love them he would not have created them. They pray to him because of their conviction that he loves them. In African traditional life one does not talk much about love; but one realises love through the things that one receives, and in this case God's love is experienced through his creation and provision of life, rain, health, protection, etc. God heals the sick (ch. 3) and saves or protects in time of danger and adversity (chs. 4 and 6). He may also punish with sickness or drought (28, 246) or death (265, 267). But by far he is the God of blessings and prosperity (chs. 3, 4, and 13). Indeed these prayers are addressed to him because he is kind, loving, blessing to people. He is the Giver of all good things (56, 71, 194, etc.). He forgives man (lets 'the shortcomings and failings lie down', 235, 237b, 238); and in prayer of purification he is asked to remove the offence and 'Put it in a deep pit; place a stone upon it; let the good wind from the north and south and from the rising to the setting sun blow upon it' (238).

In response man puts trust and faith in God as master and Lord, Creator and Father. 'We have come to thee, O Do (God), to ask for life. . . . We know thou art a strong God and have faith in thee' (23). The medicine-man prays in complete trust to him: 'Spirit, I am Thine, thou art mine, come to me!', knowing that he will help him in his work of healing: 'Thou canst do all, and without thee, I am powerless, I am powerless' (77). The people invoke him at their yearly festival, as 'Thou our Lord' (21), asking him to cause it to rain so that they and their herds may live and their fields produce good harvests. They fall before him as their Chief and Preserver making a sacrifice to him (195). He is their Master to whom they dedicate a new baby (199); their Lord to whom one promises to give another sacrifice when he heals the sick (227). Animals—sheep, goats and cattle—are sacrificed to him, and a variety of offerings made to him (ch. 10). Man has complete trust and confidence in God, and makes credal statements about his faith in God (ch. 11).

Such then, briefly, is the picture of God as it emerges from these prayers. It shows him to be personal, approachable, loving, kind, giver and preserver of life, and the Father who creates all things. In praying to God, people's attitudes are summed up in the words of one prayer: 'Oh God of our forefathers, all our lives depend on you and without you we are nothing' (249).

The spirits are the second category of spiritual realities which emerge in these prayers. There is absolutely no question that African peoples, as a whole, are very much aware of the reality of spirits (or at least realities, besides God, which fall into the spiritual realm). People address these realities, or make mention of some of them, in several of their prayers. We would estimate that about ten per cent of the prayers are addressed to the spirits or make mention of them in one form or another. Chapter 8 is made up of a collection of prayers addressed to the spirits, but reference to them occurs in some of the other chapters as well. As there is a further commentary in chapter 8, we do not need to go into details of the spirits here.

We know that in African religion it is held that some of the spirits were created as such by God, others are the remaining portion of departed people, and some are personifications of natural objects and phenomena. The prayers as they stand do not make this distinction clear, but they are addressed chiefly to the living dead of the family (who may be mentioned by name), or to personifications; and hardly to spirits which are unknown or not connected with the family.

The spirits are innumerable, 'thronging together like swarming mosquitoes in the evening' (146). Some are called 'friendly ones' (48), being part of the family, and are asked to help; but some may cause havoc to people if they are spirits of persons who were killed in battle or unjustly (58). As a rule 'the spirits of our fathers' are friendly to people (58), they are greeted and summoned to receive libation, offerings and sacrifices which are made as acts of remember-bering them. 'Let the great ones gather' (35), people invoke them; and remind them that if they do not help in time of distress (barren-ness), 'your name and ours shall be forgotten upon the earth' (124). In inviting the living dead to receive an offering, people show clearly that for them the spirits are real: 'Your food is here, here it is. . . . Today we give you blood, here it is. . . . Today we have cooked (a feast) for so-and-so, Today we have given him meat' (150). People even comfort the spirits (living dead) who may feel as though they have been neglected: 'If the other spirits are laughing at you, you may pooh-pooh them (for) they are poor; you may come, you may lick your blood, it is here' (151).

The spirits of family members who have departed, the living dead as we call them, are the ones that feature most in the prayers. They are spirits of the grandfathers and grandmothers, spirits of deceased parents and other relatives, spirits of deceased wives, husbands or children. They are family spirits going back four or five generations, and the living are conscious about the need to remain on good terms with these spirits. Therefore the living perform acts of remembrance, in form of offering small amounts of food and beverage, or occasionally sacrificing chickens, goats and sheep. Indeed, many of the approaches made to these family spirits are in the context of offerings of foodstuff (ch. 8). The departed must be remembered by the living (33, 34, 35, 124, 150, 151, 191, 254, etc.), otherwise people feel uncomfortable or attribute some misfortunes to their neglect of the spirits. 'If you are such and such spirits, Release this child; See I have lighted a fire for you. See, I have given you beer and food' (34); 'Let the great ones gather! What have we done to suffer so?... Here is food, we give to you. Aid us, your children' (35). In being remembered the spirits should also remember people: 'The promise that you promised, you of my father, where is it?' (36, cf. 124); 'O fathers and ancestors, and all who are of the near and far past, bear withness: we cry to Thee (God) to let this child be safely born' (126).

People may sometimes converse with the living dead as though in a face-to-face confrontation, even if the conversation is a mono-logue since we do not hear what the departed reply: 'Your food is here, here it is. Let the children have good health. Their wives, let them have children, So that your names may not be obliterated' (150); 'Spirits, you may walk quickly, you may come and make your clan happy . . .' (151); 'Thy home is not here with human beings; it is with the beasts. . . . There is a babe born in this thy village, and there are babes about to be born: choose for thyself. But be not hasty in choice. . . . Before thee lie many paths: choose the one most fit for thee to travel . . .' (152); 'Let the meat not stick in your throats; Eat, you chiefs, you ancestor spirits . . .' (153). People tell the departed that 'you are neither blind nor deaf to this life we live: You did yourselves once share it' (25). Thus the living dead are familiar with this life and its experiences. To renew contact with them is most important, and people are careful to avoid any neglect of the living dead; yet at the same time they can be forgotten by people, which amounts to being 'excommunicated' (155).

People appeal to the spirits for various types of help, particularly in connection with sickness. Indeed many of the prayers addressed to the departed spirits are appeals for help in time of sickness and distress, such as 28, 35, 37, 42–48. Some sickness is thought to be caused by the living dead, as ways of indicating some displeasures with the living or reminding them to remember the departed. But appeals are made to the departed regardless of whether or not they are thought to be responsible for a particular illness.

At the same time, spirits are dependent upon people and can be at their mercy. If people neglect them, then their names are obliter-ated or forgotten (155), and this, as we have seen, is like a punish-ment to the spirits. It is people who sacrifice or make offerings to them, thus keeping them in living memory (33, 34, 42, etc.). Man can order the spirits about: 'Thy home is not here with human beings; it is with the beasts; Leopards await thee. . . . Away to thine own, and let them welcome thee!' (152); 'See, I have lighted a fire

for you. See, I have given you beer and food. Eat and be content'
(34). The spirits can annoy or irritate people; therefore, people tell
them to 'Improve: else we will forget you. . . . For whose good is it
that we make sacrifices and celebrate the praises? You bring us
neither harvests nor abundant herds. You show no gratitude whatever for all the trouble we take. . . . We are angry with you!' (155);
or warn the spirits: 'What else must I do, in your opinion? Have
patience. . . . If you hinder me in any way, will you then perhaps
receive anything? Never!' (156). The spirits are invited or summoned
by man: 'Let the great ones gather. . . .' (35); 'Here is our food. All
you spirits of our tribe, invite each other. . . . Come, all of you, to
eat this food' (189).

Man can send the spirits away as he wishes: 'You, spirit, you
must leave this person alone. . . . Come, I will take you to your
body' (158), 'Go and don't return' (157, 152 cf. ch. 8). When the
spirits become notorious, people exorcise them (38, 157, 158, 161,
163); and if there is need they remove the spirits from one place to
another (164, 165). People may address the spirits in a stern manner:
'. . . my father: Why did you go to earth and keep silence? Was not
this your house before? When evil comes to your house, why do
you not pray to God?' (254). But paradoxically, man also takes a
posture of respect towards the spirits of one's elders or other
respected persons, particularly in time of need: 'We can only speak
your names, We cry to you for help' (42); 'What is it, chiefs? I
want to be well. Here then, is the thing I am giving you' (46, cf. 44,
45, 47, 48).

People make offerings and sacrifices, in certain cases, to the
spirits, especially the living dead. There are many examples of this
practice, which is carried out in time of need or when people are
eating and drinking (in which case the offerings are tokens of hospitality and remembrance towards the departed). See, among others,
28 (water offered to the grandparents), 33 (fire lighted for the spirit),
34 (beer and food given to the spirits, and a fire lighted), 35 (food),
40 (sacrifice of a sheep), etc. Spirits are associated with certain
diseases or misfortunes (33, 34, 163) and appeal is made to them at
times in general sickness: 'If you do not heal him Who will prepare
the feast, The feast of initiation for you?' (34); 'O thou Gumede!
O thou Mputa! Here is your beast: That your child may be healed'
(42; cf. 30, 34, 35, 36, 38, 39, 40). People petition spirits for good
things: 'Your food is here, here it is: Let the children have good
health, Their wives let them have children. . . . Let us have good

health. . . . Lions and leopards, let them be killed. . . .' (150, cf. 153, 154, 156, 182, 185, 196, 254). Spirits can get angry or displeased with people (47, 124), but rarely would people take their experiences to be punishment from the spirits (cf. 35, 39, 41).

In a very few cases we get prayers addressed to spirits of the earth, trees and animals (164, 165, 167). The majority of prayers to the spirits are addressed to departed members of the family, or some major tribal leaders. Personification of natural objects and phenomena is found in some of the prayers, in which case the object concerned is itself (and not a spirit) addressed. The best example of this personification is prayer 68 which is addressed to the earth, the forests, the trees, the rivers and streams: 'Conspire together, O earth and rivers: conspire together O earth and rivers and forests. Be gentle and give us plenty from your teeming plenty . . .' (cf. 89, 90, 111, 145).

Besides the spirits that we have so far discussed, there are divinities or national heroes to whom prayers are very occasionally addressed or whose names are mentioned in prayers. These are, however, extremely few, and include Kunda of the Ngombe (31, 271, 272, 275, 276), Nyikang of the Shilluk (215, 230, 256), Macardit, Garang, etc., of the Dinka (37, 182, 229), and a few others (cf. 42, 114, 131, 149, 264). The role of these divinities is hardly clear from the prayers. Kunda is mentioned more or less unconsciously (31, 271, 272, 275, 276) and in the prayers themselves we do not know who he was or is. Only Nyikang is something like a national intermediary: 'O Nyikang, call upon God . . .' (215, cf. 230) and is closely associated with God (256, cf. 230).

It emerges clearly that even though people mention or address the spirits when praying, it is almost exclusively within the family circle that the spirits have any significance as far as prayers are concerned. In many cases the references to the family spirits are made as acts of remembering the living dead, or as appeals in times of sickness or other family distress. Some of the prayers are addressed simultaneously to God and the spirits. Prayers or references to the so-called 'nature spirits' are extremely rare and virtually non-existent, as are also prayers to divinities and national or tribal heroes. The spirits hardly play the role of intermediaries even on the family level. Instead, they are requested to help, when need be, or simply told about the state of the family and then expected to assist, not because they have special powers but simply as part of their respective families. On national affairs no prayers are addressed to the spirits: they are directed to God, just as the overwhelming majority of the other prayers are also directed to him whether on a personal, family or regional level. Although the spirits have a comparatively small role in the prayers, people nevertheless feel attached to them in a way that they do not seem to feel attached to God who is their Creator, Father and Keeper. There is only a small gap between people and the spirits which is bridged through kinship ties and acts of remembrance; but the gap between the people and their Creator is enormously great. People know that when they die they become spirits; but there is no possibility in African religion that when they die they would share in the divine nature of their Creator.

The role, nature and position of *intermediaries*, if any, do not emerge clearly in these prayers. The majority of the prayers have absolutely no intermediate figures between the speaker, man and the addressee, mainly God. People take the position of being heard directly by God or the other spiritual realities, in which case there is no need for intermediaries. In prayer 264, the clan divinity 'Great Gourd of my father' is expected to help the needy man who is left alone, but it is not necessarily to convey requests from men to God or to bridge the two parties. We have seen that Nyikang of the Shilluk is a national link between men and God, but even then he is more so in a mythological sense than in the day-to-day experiences of the people (215, 256, cf. 230). Kunda of the Ngombe is mentioned only as a formula in opening or closing prayers (31, 271, 272, 275, 276).

Where mention is made of one's forefathers, they are simply requested to help or hear people's prayers, without necessarily relaying them to God or liturgically bridging the gap between man and God (e.g., 25, 35, 126, 254). We have one prayer (237a) in which a diviner-priest makes confession to God on behalf of an offender, who then takes up his own prayer as well and asks for forgiveness.

On the basis of the prayers available here, we may rightly conclude that African peoples do not place intermediaries between man and God or man and other spiritual realities. When man prays, he prays directly, even if he may appeal simultaneously to both God and these other realities. Prayer is a direct and personal communication between man and whatever spiritual realities he chooses to address. Even if realities other than God may be addressed or mentioned in at least ten per cent of the prayers, such realities are not intermediaries between man and God and man seems to bring them into the picture primarily for ontological purposes.

MAN

We come now to consider the picture of man himself as it emerges from these prayers. We keep in mind, however, that this is a liturgical and not comprehensive picture: we are seeing man at prayer, man communicating with God and other spiritual realities. It is, therefore, in a sense, a spiritual picture of man painted by himself while posing at a religious moment.

In a note of humility, man calls himself God's 'small worm' (13), and an 'ant' (115, 232). He is as a child before God and the departed (28, 42, 276). He has no strength in the presence of the Almighty God: 'Today we, your creatures, prostrate ourselves before you in supplication. We have no strength' (66); and 'Thou canst do all, and without Thee, I am powerless' (77). Man is also a wrongdoer and thereby causes pain to himself: 'We make this sacrifice in order to have rain . . . . We are wrongdoers. If one of us engages in strife today, if one of us sheds blood, we will not have rain' (168; cf. 246). Man is utterly unlike God, his position being on the earth below just as God's position is high up: 'God is on high, Man is below. . . . Each to himself, each in his dwelling' (242).

Man considers himself, however, to belong to God. For that reason he refers to God as Father, Creator, Maker, when addressing him in many of the prayers. People speak of themselves as 'the children of God' or 'the people of God'. Therefore they pray: 'I know that the Father will help me' (10); 'What is all this for, O God? Alas, I am your child' (232); 'My Father forgive me, I have killed' (the sacred animal, 237b), etc. Indeed it is because man considers himself to be in a child-parent relationship with God that he prays to God. Man is utterly dependent on God for food, rain, prosperity, health, children, life and shelter. Therefore he prays for all the things for which he depends on God and to a much smaller extent on other spiritual realities. For this reason man prays: 'O God of our forefathers, all our lives depend on you and without you we are nothing. . . . Without you we can't live because we shall have no food or water to drink. You are the source of life' (249). In another credal statement he says: 'I know that worshipping God Makes it rain when there is a drought' (250). Therefore, man must constantly implore God for life: 'Come all and implore God to give life to Man, Come all and receive life from God' (239).

Man's earthly life is, however, fleeting. He is not immortal here. 'Man is born, he eats and sleeps. He fades away, And then comes the great cold. . . . Man is gone, the prisoner is freed, The shadow has disappeared' (141). Realizing the brevity of life, he addresses the newly dead relative: 'Prepare a place for us, In a little while we shall reach, Let us reach each other' (142). So man suffers the agonies of death, and wishes that God would have it otherwise: 'O great Nzambi (God), what thou hast made is good, but thou hast brought a great sorrow to us with death. Thou shouldest have planned in some way that we would not be subject to death' (143). Yet death is not the end, for man continues to exist in the spirit form. We have already discussed the question of spirits. But this belief in the continuation of life is no special comfort to the living. Death is painful, it is terrorizing, it is tormenting and grievous (138f). Therefore people will pray and sacrifice to God and some-times to other spiritual realities in order to be healed or remain in good health (ch. 3).

Man is not afraid when he trusts God (218). Indeed, he prays to God in complete confidence and trust, and we have many statements of real confidence in God. Man believes that God listens to him, sees him and takes care of him even when he dies: 'God, you have called too soon! Give him water, he has left without food; Light a fire, he must not perish' (142). For this reason man commends a dying person: 'Our God, who has brought us (to this world), May she take you!' (139).

In these prayers we see man blessing, and very occasionally pronouncing a solemn condemnation on evil-doers. We see man as a weak creature in the sight of God, yet at the same time confident and trusting because he is the child of God. In the prayers man addresses God as his Father, Creator, Protector, Provident. Man acknowledges spiritual realities of which God is supreme. Man speaks to these realities, addressing nine-tenths of his prayers to God and one-tenth to the other invisible realities. The items for which he prays range considerably from personal requirements like health, children and wealth, to national and universal needs like happiness and peace. Thus, man is concerned with both his physical and spiritual welfare. He wants to be in harmony with the world in which he is living. For that reason he is, as it were, the priest of the universe: he is the chief agent for spiritualizing the physical and for making corporate the spiritual through his prayers and rituals.

In praying, man takes on different postures and makes certain promises. He is confident because he is praying: 'Death does not come to him for whom prayer is made' (91); 'Spirit, I am thine and thou art mine' (77). His heart is generally clean morally and spiritually: 'I have no sin upon my soul' (78), otherwise he would not be addressing God. 'We are but little children Unknowing anything evil' (28), he feels. He is certain that God will respond to his prayers: 'He will grant it' (98) is the chorus by which people express their conviction that the requests which are being sent to God will be granted. He regards God as the One 'upon whom men lean and do not fall' (135), and in praying he is certain that he will not fall. So, when he prays for a sick child, he ends the prayer: 'And thou wilt grant me my desire' (27). Though death may threaten him, he is sure that God will intervene and give him life: 'Come all and implore God to give life to Man' (239). (See ch. 11.)

Yet at times, the individual man feels the pains and agonies of this life, and almost despairs. 'As for me, Imana (God) has eaten me, yo-ho-o! As for me, he has not dealt with me as with others' (119). In frustration he gets so angry with God that he threatens to kill him: 'I don't know for what Imana (God) is punishing me: if I could meet with him I would kill him!... If only I could meet you and pay you out! Come on, let me kill you! Let me run you through with a knife! O Imana, you have deserted me! Yo-ho-o' (120). Thus, at the height of his agony, man feels as though God has deserted him, for to be without God is to perish indeed.

In a number of prayers, people make promises to God or the spirits. These are anticipatory promises, and there are many of them. In prayer 60, if God makes man find honey, man will bless him again. If a son is born, the father will offer a goat as a sacrifice (125). If the spirits watch over someone they are told that 'you will receive your due' (156). When benefits come, a cow and beer will be offered in return (255), and sea-shells will be given to God when or if he protects a sick person from death (23). Similarly, when a sick child recovers, the forefathers will receive a sacrifice (47). People will remember the departed and shout their glory if prosperity comes according to prayer 62. Even the earth, in personification, is promised a sacrifice: 'Soon we shall redden your bosom with blood' (68). There are other examples of these promises (94, 124, 140, 203, 227, cf. 228). In making the promises, man shows his gratitude towards the spiritual realities, as well as his concern that they grant him his request urgently. The promises are a kind of covenant that man makes with God and the spirits. This strengthens man's earnestness and sincerity in his prayers.

We also see man assembled for prayer, for making offerings and sacrifices to the spiritual realm. Such assemblies are the height of community participation since they bring together the living and sometimes the departed, to make a united outreach towards the spiritual realm, to communicate with the spiritual realities, and thus affirm a oneness between the physical and the spiritual. A good number of the prayers involve a recitation by one person and a response by the other people present for the occasion. This is a sign of harmony among those who are praying. It is also an expression of corporate faith, corporate religiosity, and a solidification of the group consciousness.

THINGS PRAYED FOR

There is a very wide variety of things for which these prayers are made. Each prayer has its own purpose even if these purposes can be grouped as we have done under the different chapters. Innumerable prayers ask for children (e.g., 55, 56, 57, 61, 118, 120, 124) since this is one of the chief concerns of African peoples. A marriage which does not produce children becomes miserable unless other arrangements are made to get children, for example through the marriage of additional wives if the first wife is barren, or through fathering children by a close relative (brother) if the husband is the one who is unable to bear. The agonies of being childless are painfully expressed in prayer 118 among others: 'O Imana (God) of the country of the Hutu and the Tutsi, if only you would help me just this once! O Imana, if only you would give me a homestead and children! . . . I cry to you: Give me offspring, give me as you give to others! Imana, what shall I do, where shall I go? I am in distress: where is there room for me? O Merciful, O Imana of mercy, help this once!'

There are also many prayers for healing, health and life in chapter 3. These items are universal needs of man everywhere. Man is always afflicted with various types of illness and threat to his life. Therefore he prays to be protected from death, to be healed in sickness, to be saved from danger. The prayers in this category show an intensification of people's concerns with central needs of life.

Prayers for prosperity in chapter 4 mention children, cattle, sheep, and goats as constituting essential values of people. To have these things is to be truly rich and prosperous, and the family that has them is happy. In this connection, too, are prayers for victory in war or success in cattle raid, and deliverance from adversity (ch. 6). African peoples, like other societies of the world, have been involved in wars and fightings with one another and with enemies from the outside. For this reason we have many prayers connected with wars (ch. 6) which, naturally, ask for victory over one's enemy, protection while at war, and comfort when war breaks out. War prayers are very much one-sided since they are concerned with getting what is good for one's group and what is evil for the opponents.

Rain is another key item and there are so many prayers for it that we have devoted chapter 9 to them. Rain prayers are never offered on a private personal or family basis: they are always community centred. 'We make this sacrifice in order to have rain' (168); 'God, have-we-prayed-to-Thee, Give us rain' (173); 'We come to ask for water—We who are dying from thirst' (178). Rain prayers are offered by the whole community, for the whole community and with the support of the whole community. Indeed, rain is so important that when it comes it is as though God himself were visiting people with personal blessings: 'Come to us with a continued rain, O Lesa (God), fall!' (170), they plead with God. In case of a dangerous storm, people would also pray that God may keep away the storm (179, 180, 181).

Some prayers ask for success in undertakings, such as hunting, healing, fishing, travelling and, as we have seen, fighting. The medicine-men or diviners pray for success in their work (77–80). The hunters recite a litany or invocation for success (85–87), as does the fisherman (88, 89) and the traveller (90, 91). In this same spirit are prayers for good harvest (66–75) and the thanksgiving which goes with it.

Over twenty short formulas of blessings are included here (280–283) for personal needs (e.g. protection, good fortune, success, peace, safety, children, and longevity); and several blessings for individuals, communities, nations and mankind (269–279). Blessings are reckoned in terms of material prosperity (269), long life (270, 283), protection (271), safety (272), fertility and good health (273, 282), victory (275, 277), life and vitality (278), happiness and peace (279, 284–288), rain (ch. 9), etc.

There are some few prayers which ask for the removal of evil or troubles (61, 110), of witchcraft (108, 109), of impurity or wrongdoing (237, 238) and of a curse (267). There are prayers of purification where wrongdoing has been done, as well as where people want purity, dedication, newness, and removal of, or keeping away from, ritual impurity (183–187, 238). It is clearly noticeable, however, that these prayers do not concern themselves with 'sin' in the sight of God, except in an implicit manner in a very few cases (235, 236, 237). People approach God without feeling that they are in any way sinners or wrongdoers in his sight: they pray to him because he is their Father and they are his children.

There are prayers of thankgiving, praise and rejoicing which we have grouped together in chapter 12. These are well introduced by prayer 251: 'I shall sing a song of praise to God: Strike the chords upon the drum. . . .' These prayers do not concern themselves with asking: instead, they are a record of people's feeling of joy and gratitude towards God for what He has done for them: 'Thou, O Tsui-goa, O that we may praise Thee, That we may give Thee in return!' (257). At this point, man is overwhelmed and he makes a stammering gesture towards the majesty of God: 'O, my Father, great Elder, I have no words to thank you . . . O my Father, when I look upon your greatness I am confounded with awe' (259). He dances for joy before God (260, 263).

Man also prays for harmony with nature (trees, rivers, animals and the earth) as shown in prayers 68 and 69, and with the departed (ch. 8). Individuals ask for miscellaneous personal items like the hungry man who prays that he would find something to eat (112, cf. 113), the hunter who asks for a springbok (111), the traveller that sunset be delayed so he may arrive before it is dark (90), the diviner-priest trainee who prays that he would not 'become impotent' and that his sexual urge would not make a slave of him (76), etc.

Thus, the items mentioned in these prayers have a personal dimension, a community orientation and a universal application. The prayers are, therefore, very comprehensive in their scope, and they scan a vast range of people's experiences and reflections.

CONCEPTS OF GOOD AND EVIL

Among other things in these prayers there emerge contrasting, yet related, concepts of good and evil. We shall briefly examine these two concepts which are bound up with the items prayed for.

Good is conceived in many forms. Praying is itself good. The ruination of the land is attributed to failure to pray to God (214) whereas calling upon God produces rain (blessings, 215, 250) and causes the barren woman to give birth (250). It is good because God the Creator will listen when people pray (216), and when one takes

God to oneself the enemies are frightened (223). It is a joyful thing, therefore, to pray: 'Let us lift our voices in prayer, Offering up an ox to the Creator' (226); and all are summoned to assemble for prayer: 'O men and children, come along, pray to God!' (231). The one who prays is happy: 'O Father, Creator, God, I ask Thy help. . . . To Thee in time of the new moon, I address my plea. . . . Come all and implore God to give life to Man, Come all and receive life from God' (239). In the confessional-creed which states who is a true human being, it is clearly indicated that he is a religious person who performs sacrifices and prays so that miracles happen (250).

Peace and peaceful rest are important elements of what is good. Therefore people refer to them in many prayers (28, 45, 47, 49, 68, 69, and ch. 13). Peace here means freedom from worry, disease, hunger, danger and death. It also means having joy, happiness, tranquillity, harmony, good health, and many children.

Good is experienced in form of recovery from illness and escape from death (27, 28, 29). It is abundance of life and increase of life (23, 25, 26, 207), fertility and increase of children (124).

Purity from taboos (183) is good, as is also the purity of the home (185), purity from witchcraft or witches (187), and purity of marriage according to accepted practice (184). Therefore newly-built houses are consecrated (204, 205, 206), the royal stool is sprinkled and blessed (207), the newly-forged sword is blessed (208), the beer-trough is dedicated to God (210), as are also a new homestead and a new year (211, 212). In the same concern for purity, children are dedicated or presented to God (199, 200), initiation candidates are consecrated before circumcision (201), and the individual commits himself to the divinity (202, 203).

Love is good and sharply contrasts with hatred. The dying man prays: 'And though I behold a man hate me, I will love him' (140); and another person invokes: 'A man who hates me, let him depart from me; A man who loves me, let him come to me' (264). Obedience to one's parents is good (105, 234). It is good to hold no malice towards other people (49). Harmony is good among one another, between people and the living dead (124, 156), and between man and nature (68, 69). Success and prosperity are good, as shown in many prayers. Coolness is a symbol of good (48, 240, though not in prayer 141 where it is the symbol of finality and death).

Evil is conceived in various ways, but it is generally the absence or opposite of good. Hatred is evil (140) just as love is good. The curse is evil (265, 267, 268) just as blessings are good and sought

for. Therefore the curse is used as a weapon for inflicting severe
punishment upon the thief (265, 266) and those who curse others
(267, 268). Theft is evil and it is generally dealt with very severely
(265, 266) so that when thieves are caught they are often beaten
even to death. Witchcraft is another hated element in African life,
though there are not many prayers here that mention or deal with
it. The hunters fear that witchcraft will frustrate their efforts and
they must find this out before they set off (85); and those who
bewitch others are to be killed (108, 109).

Adultery is considered to be evil in one prayer (9), and a diviner-
priest prays that he does not become a slave to his sexual urge (76).
But to become impotent is a terrible evil (76). To offend against
one's parents is morally evil (9). When the departed are neglected,
this is bad and people may interpret subsequent misfortunes as
resulting from such negligence (cf. 155).

Illness is evil: it spoils the land (49). But death is the worst form
of evil, and man struggles to delay it, keep it away, or even declares
categorically that 'We have refused death this day' (49). Prayers that
deal with illness, sickness and death are innumerable. The agony
that comes with death is almost unbearable (138–149). In the face
of death we see man at his weakest point of existence, reduced to
the lowest level of life, and made as helpless as a tadpole in a dry
pond. The funeral recitation in 141 recollects the inevitability of
death: 'The creature is born, it fades away, it dies, And comes then
the great cold. . . .' In prayer 143 the bereaved wish, in desperation,
that God would 'have planned in some way that we would not be
subject to death. O Nzambi (God) we are afflicted with great
sadness.'

Shortage of rain, drought, famine, hunger, shortage of food and
water, all these are experienced as forms of physical evil. Several
prayers make mention of them (112, 113, 114, and chapter 9 which
has prayers specifically for rain).

To be without children and a home is a form of evil which is very
hard to bear. Thus one who has neither a home nor children moans:
'O Imana (God), if only you would give me a homestead and
children! I prostrate myself before you, Imana of Urundi (Ruanda).
I cry to you: Give me offspring, give me as you give to others. . . .
Where shall I go? I am in distresss: Where is there room for me?'
(118). We have seen other prayers for fertility and children. Failure
to bear children even if through nobody's fault brings great shame
and misery to the individuals and families concerned.

Thus, good and evil are daily experiences in the lives of people. They pray for the increase of the good and the removal of the evil. The ultimate good comes from God; and it is also God who may remove evil. Prayer 240 summarizes this position very adequately: 'Our Father, it is thy universe, it is thy will, let us be at peace, let the souls of the people be cool; Thou art our Father, remove all evil from our path'.

SOME LITERARY FEATURES

One of the outstanding features of these prayers is the poetical form which most of them take. This is probably the result of their long usage which has given them the most suitable form for memorization and recitation. Some of them are sung, often by the leader while the rest of the people respond with a given formula or by repeating some of the words of the leader. The poetical prayers have a powerful rhythm, which has not been lost even through translation into English. These prayers are indeed a valuable source of traditional poetry and have all the qualities of good poetry: imagery, rhythm, vividness, use of figures of speech and symbolism, concentration of meaning, and the feeling which touches the innermost parts of one's being.

We take, as an illustration of these poetical qualities, prayer 58. This is a prayer-song of praise for victory. It is so vividly portrayed that one almost sees and touches the victorious warriors: 'We have winnowed them as the chaff which falls from the basket' is beautiful imagery depicting the way in which the enemies have fallen before the victors. It continues: 'They fall *pum* like ashes thrown on a midden.' It is painful to hear that 'Their wives are widowed and their daughters are fatherless. . . . There is sorrow for the empty homestead, for the cattlesheds that are silent, wherein is no lowing of oxen, and the dung fires burn low and are extinguished.' Repetition comes to strengthen the power of the lines and the feelings being expressed: 'It is well', and 'We have winnowed them as the chaff which falls from the basket and they are dead'. One 'sees' the fallen dead through the vividness of the words: 'They lie in great heaps'; and one feels the sorrows of the defeated villagers: 'Their villages are desolate and the death cry is caught from house to house, from river to river.' In another prayer, 101, one can hear the battle sound through the vividness which is expressed: 'God! God! tear out. . . . Girls, be not silent. . . . Tear out, tear out.'

The repetition of the words 'And comes then the great cold' in prayer 141 is a forceful way of reiterating the brevity of life. The assembled people also repeat: 'It is the great cold of the night, it is the dark.' This also is very powerful and expressive, emphasizing the coldness and darkness of death. Even single invocations of one or two lines, as in 5, 7, 8, 52, 53, 54, 93, 170, 217, etc., are very effective as expressions of concentrated feelings and wishes. Thus, 'God give us to drink milk' (8) is a complete prayer in itself and fully summarizes the wishes of the people. So also are other brief invocations: 'God give us health' (5), or 'God! give us the belly which is good' (52), or 'Our enemies approach. O God, fortify our arms, grant us strength' (93). Here the prayer is articulated more in a cry of appeal than in an argument of words.

It is impossible to summarize the structure of these prayers since each has its own and some of the structures do not conform to any given or common form. On the whole, however, we observe that a number of the prayers open with a declaration of some truth or belief, followed by a word of praise or thanksgiving. Then the central purpose is made known, after which a statement is given to the effect that one has trust that the request will be granted. We can take prayer 27 as an illustration of this type of structure:

1   O God, thou art great,
2   Thou art the One who created me,
3   I have no other
4   God, thou art in the heavens,
5   Thou art the only One;
6   Now my child is sick
7   And thou wilt grant me my desire

Lines 1–3 make a declaration of faith and fact; lines 1, 4, and 5 are statements of praise. Line 6 presents the request, and line 7 affirms that the request will be granted.

There are, also, many prayers which present the request at the very beginning and contain no statements of faith or fact or thanksgiving. This only underlines our observation that there is no given structure in these prayers.

SPIRITUALITY

We have already touched on various aspects of the spirituality contained in these prayers. Here we shall only summarize and reiterate some of the points. Spirituality is probably the greatest religious value of these prayers. They are the outpourings of man's soul and spirit in the direction of the divine, the spiritual realm and its values. But spirituality is a difficult word to define, and we shall here apply the word collectively to mean those values that go to satisfy or cultivate the part of man which communicates with or reaches towards the spiritual realm. These prayers contain spiritual values and those who recite them do so in a spiritual attitude of a spiritual direction.

Purity, cleanliness of heart, and holiness as spiritual values are mentioned or implied in a number of prayers: 9, 78, 183–186, 239, 265 and 266. Man is approaching God in prayer, and man believes that God is holy, pure, and 'clean'. Man must aspire to be clean also, as he declares in 78: 'Since I have never taken anything from others, I stole nothing. . . . I have no sin upon my soul.' Therefore people offer prayers of purification (chapter 10), even if they desire to be purified from ritual blemishes rather than from any sins committed before God, and to purify marriage, a new home, a fire and witches.

Humility of man before God and the spiritual realm is an element of spirituality. Man feels that he is an ant (58 and 232) or a small worm (13). He needs help from God and the departed. Therefore he humbles himself in asking for that help. When man calls upon God as Father, man is taking the humble position of children before their parents, but this is a position of sonship or childhood and not of servanthood. It is a position of humble love, respect, honour, and even admiration or adoration from man towards God and sometimes the living dead.

Trust, faith, confidence and assurance are evident in many prayers. Indeed it may be said that without trust or faith in the spiritual realm, man would not offer prayers. The prayers are made blindly as far as the physical eyes are concerned; but man prays with his eyes of faith wide open. Prayer is an exercise in confidence, and in praying man moves in word, ritual, hope, and trust towards the spiritual. Chapter 11 contains many prayers which bring this confidence to the forefront, though all the other prayers also have their element of confidence. 'Though the tribe holds a feast against me I shall not fear' (218) is one of the many declarations of trust. We see similar trust in the prayer for a safe journey (91): 'Death does not come to him for whom prayer is made; death comes only to him who trusts in his own strength!' This statement draws a sharp contrast between the man who prays and the man who does not pray. The one who prays trusts in God and, occasionally, other spiritual realities, whereas the one who does not pray trusts in himself and is subject to trouble. (Further reference can be made to prayers 172, 218–222, 263 and the commentary on chapter 11.)

Peace is another spiritual element which occurs frequently in the prayers (28, 144, 224, 284–285). Peace carries with it the sense of tranquillity, quietness, freedom from disease and danger, satisfaction, contentment, happiness, and removal of all forms of evil. People pray for it as one of the greatest blessings obtainable. Indeed there is no satisfaction without peace. It goes with happiness (287), and it is necessary upon people, animals and crops (285, 286). The final prayer in this collection is one for universal peace: 'May peace reign over the earth' (288), since this is the crown of man's spiritual aspirations.

Love (140, 147), care (142), tenderness and gentleness (126, 127, 138, 142 and 144) come out in several prayers, as spiritual elements of high quality. The dying man prays that he would love even those who hate him (140). The living are so concerned about the welfare of their departed that they ask God to look after him: 'God, you have called too soon! Give him water, he has left without food; Light a fire, he must not perish' (142). The midwife prays for the newly born baby in characteristic tenderness: 'I take you out of the world of the spirits. Do not be sick, settle down. . . . Here is this cloth for you, and now a pillow and now a bed. . . . Settle down . . .' (127). The bereaved pray: 'Let us weep softly over him, in peace. Let us help each other in our pain . . .' (144), bringing out the most tender feelings of the human heart.

Deep sorrow makes people feel as if God has abandoned them, and they can hardly face such a state of living without God. Prayers 116–120 capture something of this feeling of apparent abandonment. A man cries in distress: 'My father Deng, do not forsake me, My father Deng, do not abandon me to the Powers (of sickness)' (116). If God is momentarily eclipsed, people experience this as death itself: 'God has forsaken us, The Creator of the sun refuses us life' (117). Deep sorrow makes one feel as though God consumed one, which is tantamount to being dead: 'As for me, Imana (God) has eaten me, yo-ho-o! . . . Sorrow is not to go weeping. . . . Woe is me! Yo-ho-o!' (119). Indeed one reaches such a point of desperation that one gets angry with God and threatens to kill him: 'Couldn't you give me one little child, Yo-ho-o! I am dying in anguish! If only I could meet you. . . . Let me run you through with a knife! O Imana (God), you have deserted me! Yo-ho-o! (Woe is me!)' (120). Deep sorrow and desperation reveal the other side, the dreadful side of spirituality. Yet, in spite of being so downcast and in such despair, man still prays and raises his spirit above his sorrows towards God. Man would still look upon God as the one 'upon whom men lean and do not fall' (135), their Father to whom they offer their prayers.

Man looks upon God as his refuge and sings praise to Him accordingly: 'Reign! O Lord of the cattle of the Barundi.... Reign, our refuge.... Help me to build' (255). No matter what happens, God is triumphant: 'Because I have prayed and prayed, The word of the Lord will not be mocked, His good word will ever keep thee' (220d, a prayer which has biblical undertones though there is no evidence that it is a Christian invocation).

Praise and thanksgiving are another spiritual element of great importance. There are several prayers of praise and thanksgiving (251–263) which we discuss in the commentary for chapter 12. In praise and thanksgiving the soul of man gives itself back to God, acknowledging its dependence upon him and its joy over his providence. In the same spirit we have prayers of sacrifices, offerings, dedications and consecrations, grouped together in chapter 10. These are, among other things, expressions of man's feelings of wanting to give something material, something which he owns or for which he has worked, to God and the other spiritual realities. They are acts of spiritualizing the material, and man is the executive for so doing: he mediates the physical, including himself (199–203), towards, or for, the spiritual. This giving of oneself reaches its height in prayer 77 where the medicine-man prays to God, to whom he is consecrated and pledged.

That man offers not only prayers but himself and his belongings to God and spiritual realities, shows man's confidence in the accessibility of God and the spiritual realm. People speak freely to him, without hesitation and without having to cross barriers since there are none. They call upon God at any time and in any place, for their spirit has complete access to the spiritual realm. Indeed, man feels the need to turn to God (214, 231) and cries out: 'O Shilluk, cause of the ruination of our lands; Why not turn again to God, up there? Why not turn again to the real God?' For this reason, man calls upon fellow man to pray, to 'go' spiritually to God or towards God: 'O men and children, come along, pray to God!... Pray to our God!' (231), and 'Let us lift our voices in prayer, Offering up an ox to the Creator'(226). One is happiest when one prays to God, for he is the ultimate source of satisfaction: 'My God, to thee alone I pray. . . . He Who is like a sage, To whom I offer my prayer' (222).

This idea of man moving spiritually to God reaches an almost mystical point of absorption of man in God: 'Spirit, I am Thine, Thou art mine, come to me!' (77). This trait of mysticism is a rare element in African spirituality, but there it is. It shows the direction that spirituality follows, if not the height it might attain. In a different way, people associate the blessings of rain with God so much so that when it rains it is as if God Himself were visiting them in a physical form: 'Come to us with a continued rain, O Lesa (God), fall!' (170).

The blessings which have many forms (269–283) are another way of expressing the proximity of God with people: 'May God go with you!' (281a), 'May you go with God!' (281c), 'May God walk you well!' (281g), 'May you pass the night with God!' (281h), 'May you stay with God!' (281k), etc. The presence of God with people is the greatest blessing of which they can think and for which they can hope. To have God is to have all. God is the purity of blessings and where he is consciously felt to be, there is also an abundance of them. People are happy, therefore, to pray that God would stay with them: 'Pu! Thou, God, hast come upon us. We accept thee. Stay, stay thou with us favourably' (129). In this presence of God, man feels completely naked, open, and free to address him, and in speaking to God man acquires or generates spiritual vitality so that, for example, he can summon the impossible to happen: 'I am an absolutely true *Mukamba* (African, human being), Who knows that religious rites cause a baby to be born . . . And knows how to sacrifice in order that it may rain. . . . I know that a barren wife Can give birth when rites are performed . . . And I know that worshipping God Makes it rain when there is a drought' (250). And this might well be the ultimate experience of prayer: to enable man to penetrate into the impossible, indeed into the divine and the spiritual realm, while he is still in his physical life.

2 *Prayers for the day, the month, and the year*

Of the prayers offered regularly or seasonally, the largest number we have has to do with the morning period. There are nine morning prayers in our collection. Man wants to start the day with fresh hopes and expectations. Therefore he prays that God will remove 'every pain, every ill', and 'let me smile in good fortune' (2) or 'bring all fortunes to me today' (4). As he goes forth to his work, he solicits God's *spittal* (blessings), which is medicine against all kinds of unknown illnesses, dangers and accidents. God is asked to protect and prosper, not only the individual but also his family and possessions, in course of the day.

Several of the morning prayers (e.g., 1, 2, 4, and 9) show a sense of, or concern for, moral-spiritual purity at the start of the day. God is asked to 'take away from us . . . every ill' (1); the woman who prays in 2 tells God that she does 'not eat what is not mine' nor 'steal my neighbour's goods', she is 'never in debt' and has always a happy disposition towards other people. She has no malice towards anybody. Therefore she hopes to continue in that happy state of her inner, personal being, and of being in good relationship with other people. This is not a prayer of self-justification: rather it is a sincere exposition of her conviction that she wants to be morally upright, as God can see. In 4, the individual actually asks for God's forgiveness and washing away of 'all the evils of which I have thought throughout the night'. It is as if the dawn of day brings with it a sense of purity, holiness, sacredness. Daylight becomes a symbol of purity, and one wishes to enter the new day with a pure mind. The same concern is expressed in prayer 9, in which the person tells God that 'I am innocent'—not having 'offended against my father and my mother', or committed adultery, or stolen, in course of the previous night (when these things could have happened). Furthermore he has not killed anybody without a just cause.

This concern with moral uprightness indicates not only people's wish for peace and spiritual health, but also their conviction that if one is not upright one's prayers will not be fully effective and misfortunes may result. People want contentment, good fortune, prosperity, joy, happiness and peace.

African peoples are not shy about asking for material and physical prosperity. This comes out clearly in many of the prayers in this collection. In the morning prayers we hear the requests to God to 'bring riches today as the sun rises' and 'all fortunes' (4), and to grant food, meat, great herds and children (7, 8). Indeed three morning invocations (5, 7, 8) are for physical sustenance alone. But in addition to the material welfare, non-physical and spiritual necessities are also requested: safety, happiness, contentment, guidance, and mercy. It is not clear, however, that people consciously draw a distinction between these physical and non-physical requests, each of which is made as the occasion demands, since they are all made to 'God of my needfulness' (7).

Evening prayers are not numerous, and in our collection we have only two, one of which is for both morning and evening (11). This is rather surprising because one would have expected more praying as people enter into the period of darkness with all the fears, dangers and uncertainties associated with night. It is to be presumed, however, that more evening or night prayers exist, but these have not come to my attention. At the same time it may be that people direct their praying more to the need than to the hour of the day.

The two evening prayers we have here are too brief to give us a clear indication of people's concerns. One only tells us that someone turns to God in prayer, confident that God will help. In this, as in many other prayers, God is regarded as the Father who will undoubtedly provide safety, protection, security and all the help needed. In the other prayer (11), it is stated that God has provided 'a good day', so now he is asked also to provide 'a good night'. Exactly what is meant by 'good' is not indicated in the prayer, but we may assume that safety, health, peace and the provision of life's needs are some of the items in the mind of the people who use this daily prayer.

Neither are daily prayers numerous as far as our collection goes. By daily we mean those prayers recited regularly each day, so that in effect both evening and morning prayers fall under this same category. We have already commented on the prayer (11) offered both morning and evening by the Galla people, for a good day and a good night. The Nandi adults are reported to recite a daily prayer (12) twice, for protection both day and night. In this they affirm that they would continue to pray no matter what time of day it is. The prayer incorporates the departed who are regarded by African peoples to be still part of their surviving families. The Galla invocation (13) can be used at any time. Although short, it is nevertheless sufficient for the needs of the moment: man humbles himself so that he is like 'your small worm', he appeals to God to 'stretch your hand over him' if and when enemies arise. Enemies can be interpreted to mean human and animal sources of harm, dangers, accidents, illness and misfortunes.

Praying at meal time seems uncommon in African religion. We have only one (14) example of what may come under meal time prayers. As expected, it is a communal prayer in which one person takes the lead and others respond. The elders are in a jovial mood at a beer-drinking party. They think of their sons who are away, presumably on a journey, in a battle or cattle raid. They hope that God will protect their children, 'tie knots' so that they return home safely. This prayer is addressed to God but it is accompanied by a beer libation for the departed who are invoked to 'give us health'.

We take note of the fact that in many African societies libation and food offerings are still (although more commonly in the past) made to departed members of the family who remain in the memory of the living. These we have called the living dead. Such food and drink offerings are accompanied by prayers normally of a few words inviting the living dead to eat, drink, or hearken. Because the presence of the departed is felt to be so real, people extend their hospitality to the living dead through the symbolic meal of bits of food and drops of drink; they also say something as a recognition of the nearness and in respect of the living dead. These are acts of remembering the departed, even if their personal names may not always be mentioned specifically.

Formal sacrifices and offerings are always accompanied by prayers and invocations, as we shall see in a later chapter. These can also be termed prayers at meal times, though such are special meal times.

Two prayers in this collection are made at the time of a new moon (15, 16). Prayers for such occasions are undoubtedly common since many African societies used to mark the appearance of the new moon with festivals, offerings or other formal religious observances. In the Mensa prayer (15), the new moon is addressed. But we may reasonably assume that the sentiments are being directed to God even if he is not mentioned by name. The idea is that people want to go through a whole moon-period in joy and happiness, and to enjoy normal life (giving birth, suckling babies, coming to the end of the journey, dwelling safely in the home, and increasing the prosperity of herds and fields). Each new moon should renew what is good in life, and that is what people ask God to bring to them regularly month by month.

In the Bushman prayer (16) the moon is again personified. The fact that it is a new moon symbolizes newness of life, youthfulness, joy, happiness, rejuvenation and liveliness. The renewal of life is symbolized by the moon's apparent death and rebirth: 'you lie down and return . . . you return evermore alive'. This phenomenon is tantalizing because the moon reminds people of the story of their lost immortality: 'Did you not promise us once that we too should return and be happy again after death?' This is a painful association of the moon with the very common African mythology of man's lost immortality and rejuvenation.

Prayers at annual occasions are not numerous in our sources, though we could include here those made at sowing, harvesting and other seasonal occasions. Only a few are included in this chapter (17–20), four of which are linked together in connection with the Ashanti Yam Festival. The first of them recites that 'the edges of the years have come round', and asks that no evil be permitted 'to come upon us'. People want to enter peacefully into the new year. The second (18) is an invocation to the living dead to accept the sacrifice of a sheep and offering of wine, and thereby to share in the festival. The third (19) is in effect for strengthening the powers of the king, giving him sanction to get rid of his enemies. Similarly in the prayer (20) at which the shrine is sprinkled, the king asks for renewal of his strength so that he may defeat his enemies in war. Thus, this series of prayers is very nationalistic, aimed ultimately at the renewal of the king's power and authority—the king being the symbol of health, prosperity and good welfare for his people.

The Nama 'Yearly Killing' festival is also a national occasion but without being centred on a king. People gather to renew their call upon God, the 'Father of our fathers'. They pray for rain in order that both men and flocks may live; they pray that they may get enough food and water, and in return they will praise and bless God, their Lord. This is a face-to-face prayer, offered as it is by the children to their Father, annually when the land is dry and people are weak, needing food and water. It is a dynamic, vivid and moving prayer, lifting the people to the very presence of their 'Father of our fathers'.

The Ga prayer (22) at the annual 'Hunger-Hooting' festival is a

universal one. Man asks that 'may the year's end meet us', may he
have long life, may no misfortune meet him in the coming year and
'may we sit again'. It is a collection of blessings at the end of one
year and beginning of another. It generates hope not only for the
immediate year yet to come, but for the life's journey up to old age.

MORNING AND EVENING PRAYERS

1 Women's morning prayer[1]

Morning has risen;
Asobe [God], take away from us every pain,
Every ill,
Every mishap;
Asobe, let us come safely home.

2 Smiling in good fortune[2]

Let me smile in good fortune;
Let my children smile in good fortune;
Let my home smile in good fortune.
I do not eat what is not mine.
I do not steal my neighbour's goods.
I always wish good health to others.
I am never in debt.
He who hates me is unjust.
I am always smiling in good fortune.

3 For a happy day[3]

Po! God, may the day dawn well;
May you spit upon us the medicine
So that we may walk well!

4 For a day full of blessings[4]

O, sun,
As you rise in the east through God's leadership,
Wash away all the evils of which I have thought throughout the
    night.
Bless me, so that my enemies will not kill me and my family;
Guide me through hard work.
O God, give me mercy upon our children who are suffering:
Bring riches today as the sun rises;
Bring all fortunes to me today.

5 Morning invocation for health[5]

Asis! Kon-ech Sapon [God! give us health].

6 We rise up in the morning[6]

We rise up in the morning before the day, to betake ouselves to our labour, to prepare our harvest. Protect us from the dangerous animal and from the serpent, and from every stumbling block.

7 'God, give me milk'[7]

God of my needfulness, grant me something to eat, give me milk, give me sons, give me great herds, give me meat, O my Father.

8 For milk [success and sustenance][8]

God! give us to drink milk.

9 'There is no sin in me'[9]

Thou, O Jouk [God], who hast created all men:
Let my family be forever happy,
I have not offended against my father and my mother,
I have not sinned with my neighbour's wife,
There is no sin in me, I am innocent:
I have stolen nothing;
I have killed no one without cause.
Grant contentment to everyone of my house.

10 The evening has fallen[10]

Now that evening has fallen,
To God, the Creator, I will turn in prayer,
Knowing that he will help me.
I know the Father will help me.

DAILY PRAYERS

11 For morning and evening[11]

O God, thou hast given me a good day,
Give me a good night;
Thou hast given me a good night;
Give me a good day!

12 O God incline thine ear[12]

O God, do thou thine ear incline,

Protect my children and my kine,
Even if thou art weary, still forbear
And hearken to my constant prayer.
When shrouded beneath the cloak of night,
Thy splendours sleep beyond our sight,
And when the sky by day,
Thou movest, still to thee I pray,
Dread shades of our departed sires,
Ye who can make or mar desires,
Slain by no mortal hand ye dwell,
Beneath the earth, O guard us well.

13 Protection against enemies[13]

If enemies should come, let not your small worm die, but stretch
your hand over him.

AT MEAL TIME

14 Invocation at the elders' drinking party[14]

One elder rises and says: They will return, say, they will return.

Response: They will return.

(*After this they all sing:*)

God! tie—knots—for—us children,
That we may greet them, that we may greet them.

(*When each man has taken his calabash, he says:*)

The—spirits—our! have—we prayed—to—you.
Regard this beer.
Ye—give us health.

AT THE NEW MOON AND YEARLY FESTIVALS

15 'Be for us a moon of joy'[15]

May you be for us a moon of joy and happiness. Let the young
become strong and the grown man maintain his strength, the
pregnant woman be delivered and the woman who has given birth
suckle her child. Let the stranger come to the end of his journey
and those who remain at home dwell safely in their houses. Let the
flocks that go to feed in the pastures return happily. May you be a
moon of harvest and of calves. May you be a moon of restoration
and of good health.

16 Moon, give me your face[16]

Take my face and give me yours!
Take my face, my unhappy face.
Give me your face,
with which you return
when you have died
when you vanished from sight.
You lie down and return—
Let me reassemble you, because you have joy,
you return evermore alive,
after you vanished from sight.
Did you not promise us once
that we too should return
and be happy again after death?

17–20 At the Annual Yam Festival (Odwira Ceremony)[17]

17 *After killing a sheep for a repast for the spirits the king addresses them:*

The edges of the years have come round, we are about to celebrate the rites of the Odwira; do not permit any evil at all to come upon us and let the new year meet us peacefully.

18 *After pouring a wine or blood libation the king continues:*

Spirits of the dead, receive this wine and sheep, let no bad thing come (upon us), we are about to celebrate the Odwira ceremony.

19 *At the ceremony the king smears the Odwira seaman with* esono, *places new yams on it and says:*

Odwira of Osai Tutu, accept this wine and drink, any one who does not wish to serve you, let me get him, let me kill him, and let me throw his head (on you), Odwira.

20 *The king sprinkles the shrine with these words:*

O Bosommuru [spirit], the edges of the years have met; you were sharp but I took that thing which you abhor and touched you (with it), but today I sprinkle you with water in order that your power may rise up again. When I and my equal, some war lord or other, meet, cut off his head and give it to me; and along with the water, with which I sprinkle you, here is a sheep.

21 'Father of fathers, let us live!'[18]
At the 'Yearly Killing' festival

Thou, O Tsui-goab [God]!
Father of our fathers,
Thou our Father!
Let the thundercloud stream!
Let our flocks live!
Let us also live, please!

I am so very weak indeed
From thirst,
From hunger!
Let me eat field fruits!
Art thou not our Father?
The Father of the fathers,
Thou Tsui-goab?

O that we may praise thee!
That we may bless!
Thou Father of the fathers!
Thou our Lord!
Thou, oh, Tsui-goab!

22 At the 'Hunger-Hooting' festival[19]

Take life, take life:
May the year's end meet us,
May we live to be old,
May no black cat cross between us;
At the end of this year,
May we sit again.

3 *Life, health, and healing*

Ultimately the majority of prayers have to do with human life in one way or another. But in this collection of African prayers there are a few that specifically ask for life to be maintained, renewed, and multiplied. Many more are aimed at healing the sick and maintaining health, but these we have placed in a section of their own.

In the prayer for clinging to life (23) it may be reasonably assumed that a person is threatened with death. Therefore this is an emergency prayer, calling upon God in faith, so that, being strong, he may protect and give life. It is uttered in desperation and a humble token offering of water (probably another beverage being spoken of metaphorically as water) is made as an indication of one's sincerity. Under the emergency circumstances, a promise is made that when the person clings to life, he and his companions will make a better offering (of sea shells) and sacrifice (of a goat).

In prayer 24, the king of the Ashanti prays that his own life and that of his people may be spared and sustained in the coming year. At this formal request for the continuation of life, he sacrifices sheep and offers new yams to the spirits of former kings. Animal life is destroyed so that it may be exchanged for human life. Yet human life is spared not magically but through the provision of abundant food in the fields and protection against illness.

In African thinking, human life is not confined to its physical form alone. It extends into the realm beyond death. Therefore those who have departed are thought to be still living, even if in a form different from the present. Appeal is made to them in prayer 25, as having shared this life and being, therefore, familiar with its trials and joys. As they are 'neither blind nor deaf to this life we live', they should 'help us therefore'. However, the kind of help needed is not stated. Presumably people feel deserted by their ancestral relatives in time of dire need, and appeal to them for any possible help they may give. They even politely rebuke the departed for seeming to be blind and deaf to the trying experiences of the present life.

In asking for life to multiply through procreation into 200, 400 and 1,460 persons, as in prayer 26, a person is simply asking to be spared and beget many children. He is addressing himself to anyone in authority who has power over life and death of other people, and who is referred to metaphorically as Death. It is a prayer to let people live in peace, let them get married, bear many children and live to see their grand- and great-grandchildren. It is an extremely painful tragedy in African societies for one to die without bearing children (by one's own biological faculties or through socio-religious arrangements). Therefore whoever has power over the lives of others, whether he be the chief, king, a divinity or God himself, is requested, in the sentiments of this prayer, to allow one to reproduce in plenty. (See further the agonies of concern for procreation in prayer 49 below.)

Prayers for health and healing are bound up with those asking for life to be spared and increased. There are many of them, as one would expect. They are painful prayers because in them man is wrestling against conditions leading to death. Here man is in dire agony, and at his weakest moment. Therefore he makes himself as humble as possible, or he feels humbled by the circumstances, before God and other spiritual realities. In desperation these prayers are addressed to every possible source of help, as if to make absolutely sure that every real and imaginary source is exhausted. Therefore, in some of the prayers we do not see a sharp distinction drawn between God and the living dead (or related spirits). Under the circumstances of strain in which these prayers are offered, man simply addresses the widest possible range of spiritual realities collectively, and it is immaterial whether reference is made sometimes to the departed or to God. The purpose of the prayers is for the sick to be healed, and man appeals to the spiritual realm for such healing.

In agony, the parent whose child is sick tells God in prayer 27 that he created him and has no other origin. His desire is that his child be healed, and the man is so confident about this that he declares rather than requests that God 'will grant me my desire'. In the longer prayer for help in sickness (28), a similar pattern is to be observed, and the departed relatives are brought into the picture. God is stated to be omnipresent in heaven and earth, the creator and conserver of everything. Man does not know for sure what has caused this sickness, but he asks, nevertheless, that God should effect healing through the herbs (roots) which the patient has to take or apply. In a real agony, appeal is made to God and 'all ancestors, males and females, great and small', to help and 'have compassion on

us, so that we can also sleep peacefully'. This prayer vividly illus-
trates our observation that all possible sources of help are exploited
to make sure that the sick recover and life is spared.

Those who make the two short invocations, 29 and 30, do not
agonize over their situation. They simply ask for recovery and make
their appeal directly to God. But in the prayer of blessing the sick
(31), the leader has to be someone of a good character who has not
broken any of God's commandments, though we do not know
exactly which these are, and whose dealings are upright. This is the
man who intercedes for the sick, while the rest of the people
gathered for the occasion shout their *mokanga* (agreement). Again
the departed members are brought into the picture, in the sense
that God is acknowledged to be 'Akongo of the ancestors' and 'of
the fathers'.

The medicine-man offers a prayer (32) as he treats the sick,
indicating that God is ultimately the healer. It is a common belief
among many traditional medicine-men (doctors) that they do not
wield final power for healing the sick and only use the powers, skills,
knowledge, and medicines given to them by God. (See also the
prayer of a priest-diviner, 76). Some of them are known to include
prayer as part of their medical practice; and in addition some make
offerings and sacrifices, or perform other religious rituals, in connection with their work. In this prayer, the medicine-man even confesses
his humility that 'we do not know how to pray to God' in ways
better than those he already uses.

Prayers 33 and 34 associate the spirits with sickness, as do several
others, even if the spirits are not clearly blamed for causing sickness
as such in every case. In 33, appeal is made to the spirit [*emandwa*]
conditionally: '*if* you have made this child sick'. Normally the
diviners are consulted about the causes of sickness, and some sick-
nesses are identified as being caused by spirits who may be using
such sickness or other misfortunes to make their wishes known. In
these two prayers the officiant or parent lights a fire at the spirit
shrine, offers meat, drink and other food. Then he tells the spirit,
'see your child: let him be healed so that he may care for your
things', or promises that on recovery the patient will be initiated
into cultic service for that particular spirit. In both cases, the
parents do everything possible to fulfil whatever the spiritual powers
may be thought to wish. Man reasons with the spirits, to convince
them: 'if you do not heal him, who will prepare the feast... for you?'
This is a face-to-face confrontation with spiritual realities, and

African peoples are very conscious of such realities. Therefore they address them directly, they argue with them, they plead with them, they sometimes sacrifice or make offerings to them, and even drive them away when they become too notorious or make unbearable demands.

In prayer 35 we see again a direct contact between man in need and his departed forefathers. He summons them: Let the great ones gather.' Then he rebukes them searchingly: 'What have we done to suffer so?' and 'Wherein have we erred?' The forefathers are told that their 'children are in distress . . .'; they are given their token (food), and of them it is demanded urgently: 'Aid us, your children.' This is another prayer of urgency, and the headman who has summoned his people for the occasion of this prayer is bitterly irritated that for no apparent reason the influenza epidemic has broken out. He exercises his authority even in the direction of the spiritual realm, and orders the great ones also to assemble and do their duty of helping their children. The agony in this prayer is vividly portrayed, and one can clearly see the desperation of the people, none of whom is 'able to give a drink of water to another'.

Prayers 36 and 37 belong together. They are very personal: 'you of my father' and 'you of my mother' had, evidently, promised to help particularly in sickness and need. But the departed have not helped, they have not fulfilled their promise or what is expected of them. The man alerts the trees, grass, earth and God to be witnesses to his need and request. He and his companions have dedicated an ox, for God, or for the departed, so that it is a token of their wish for the illness to go away. They have removed the magic bundles, and have ritually exorcized the evil divinity (*Macardit*) to leave the sick. The people have done everything possible, directed by the mystical and spiritual realms, for the healing of the sick. 'Thus! My words are finished', it is now up to 'you of my father' and 'you of my mother' to help.

In prayer 38, sickness is personified. A ritual is performed in order to drive it out and send it into the bush. A black chicken and other things are placed on the ground in front of the sick man's house, and the medicine-man speaks to the sickness. He exorcizes it out of the patient, by enticing it with the chicken, kigelia fruit, thorn tree and a ritual spear. 'You come right out', he orders it, 'and leave the body of my embryo.' At this point, the sickness is treated like a spirit, in the same way as in prayers 33 and 34. By personifying people's troubles, or blaming a spirit for them, it is psychologically more effective to handle the case by driving out the spirit, exorcizing it, pleading with it, doing something to it, or making promises to it, as a practical device of treating the sick, than by simply applying herbs or medicines alone (particularly in serious cases of illness). See also prayers 38, 40, 41 and 49.

Prayer 39 addresses itself, like the previous prayer, to a personification of the plague, Omarari. Because of the seriousness of this particular disease, people pose as though they were at its mercy: the children, the lads and the girls that are, belong to Omarari, they are at its mercy and can only plead that it should 'let thy wrath cease'. Omarari is causing havoc everywhere, even among neighbouring peoples; and all people, including the chiefs, are crying because of its harassment.

The following prayers, 40 and 41, belong to one event at which a sheep is sacrificed for a sick man. His sickness is also personified and ordered to forget, that is to go away and leave the sick man alive. The departed, thought also to be involved in the sickness, are asked to 'forget'. Almost certainly the driving of the sheep into the bush is a symbolic act of driving away the sickness. The sacrifice of the sheep is also an act of 'feeding' the living dead, to keep them quiet and provide man with the opportunity of asking them to remove their sickness: 'Let the people of the dead forget.'

Prayers 42 and 43 present us with a wrestling scene between people and the spirits, over a sick woman. People present a sacrificial animal: 'Here is your beast!' That accomplished, they now expect that the sick woman will recover. In the event that it is otherwise, they tell the spirits plainly that 'she is yours, this child of yours. It is your affair'. They have presented their earnest need; but 'if she dies . . . we can only speak your names', i.e. the people will, nevertheless, continue to recite the names of the departed, even if they are defeated by them, over the sickness of the woman. Evidently the spirits do not help, and a second plea is called for. It is now addressed to one higher than the previous spiritual realities: 'O Paramount . . . why do you refuse us?' That is an agonizing, if rhetorical, question. The plea mounts up towards a climactic desperation and the agony of the people heightens as they confront their 'Father' with a face-to-face query: 'What do you say about your child?' Why do you, Paramount and Father, not help your child? What does it mean when 'we say we are your people'? The agony drives the people to the point of questioning the father-children relationship that they have with the spirit world. Their second plea ends in dismay: 'Alas, O Paramount.' In this prayer of desperation, the words Paramount and Father may be terms of addressing God. This interpretation is also supported by the fact that often the final appeal in moments of serious sickness is addressed to God. If this be the case here, then in this prayer man is wrestling with God over the critical illness of the woman.

Prayers 44, 45, and 46 express similar sentiments to 42 and 43. People present sacrificial beasts to spirits of their forefathers, here mentioned by name, and at once expect in return that the sick be healed. They 'wish peace between us', that is, they want no sickness or other disturbances which might come from the spirit world. Evidently the people in these prayers are convinced that their sick-nesses originate from the living dead as a way of making their wishes known—in this case, asking for sacrifices and offerings. Sickness becomes a channel of communication from the world of the spirits to that of men. 'What is it, chiefs?' (46) is a self-searching question, in which someone wonders what the departed want to say or wish to have, through making him sick.

It is as if people and spirits are sitting together in prayers 47 and 48, in a very friendly atmosphere. The people are very anxious over the sickness of a child and a man. The child's mother, in tears, appeals to the 'spirits of the past', telling them that her child is theirs as well, 'therefore, be gracious unto her'. Other women take up the plea and chant about the troubles of this world, and the pain which the departed experienced at one time. The mother's wish is made known: 'Let none among you be angry with me or with my child.' The other women pray that the child should grow into adult-hood, and promise that she will then 'offer such a sacrifice to you that will delight your hearts'. This is a vivid and moving litany, set like a scene from a play of men and spirits. The second prayer is introduced by the wife on behalf of her sick husband, and other relatives join her in response. Again the atmosphere is friendly, and the people show their respects towards the 'fathers of the long ago . . . (the) friendly ones'. The spirits are asked to act unanimously in a singular-plurality to 'let thy breath be cool upon his brow'. The expression about coolness occurs in a considerable number of African societies. Coolness is the symbol of peace, tranquillity, safety and good health, whereas heat or hotness is the symbol of sickness (fever), war, danger, and the like.

Prayer 49 is one of the longest in the whole collection. The Dinka and, to a less extent, their neighbours the Nuer are reported to have

unusually long prayers compared with other African peoples. It is
not possible, in our commentary, to do full justice to this prayer
which has so many interesting features. It opens with a powerful
statement to the addressees—the earth, the father's divinity and
God—that 'we have refused death this day'. People are simply not
ready or willing to let one of their number die. They want the sick
man to be healed. They have tied an ox, ready to sacrifice it but 'not
for nothing' since they expect and want their sick man to recover.
The killing of the ox (as in prayer 40) is 'to exchange your (its) life
for the man, and for the man to stay on earth and for your life to
go with the illness'. Suddenly the sickness is personified (as in
prayers 38, 40 and 41) and told, 'you illness, I have separated you
from the man. . . . You leave the man alone, you have been given
the ox called malith.'

For a while, the address to the illness is abandoned, and the man
officiating makes an autobiographical digression. He is not a
stranger, but 'a man of this land in the tribe of Apuk Jurwir here.
I am not a bastard coming with his mother. . . . If such a one prays,
he calls upon no clan-divinity . . . and he will be unable to do anything in the case of sickness.' This man is truly native-born and
has religious roots so that his prayer should be effective in case of
sickness. The officiant then turns theological: 'Nhialic (God) is
within the man who has him. The earth is spoilt (by this illness).'
It is not clear what the meaning is about God being 'within the man
who has him'. In any case God, being invisible, is certainly present in
the man of faith, the man who is sensitive enough to acknowledge him.

In a cry of command from the man who has God in him, sickness
is banished: 'Wuu, away the sickness!' To this all the people
present cry aloud, 'wuu', and move their heads and arms in the
direction away from the Dinka people, to the south, in order symbolically to send the illness there.

Now that the illness is symbolically and ritually driven away, the
officiant tells God that 'I do not want words of such sickness, that
a man should be ill'. He solemnly declares in the name of his fore-
father(s) that he means what he says about not wanting anybody to
be ill. A new wrestling now begins between him and God: 'Why is
it, O Nhialic (God), that when one son is left alive alone out of all
the children his mother bore, you do not help, that he may be in
health?' This is a deeply agonizing question, not unlike the problems
of Job in the Bible. The man feels that since only one son is left
'behind to beget children', people are justified to refuse that he be

sick and to refuse that he should die. The argument is put forward
that, since Akol (the sick man) has no sister or brother, his agnatic
line would die out gradually, unless God helps him to recover so
that he may beget children. Now, having argued out his case so
convincingly, he calls upon God as the 'Father of all people', with
the full confidence that God 'will strengthen his arm, that no evil
may befall him'.

But it is not God alone that is involved. The deceased father of
the sick man poses an agonizing problem: 'Why have you (Agany)
left your child in misery in his father's tribe? In the past, when you
were alive, you left Akol as an only child.' The departed father must
also realize that it is reasonable to help his sick son. There are other
spirits involved as well: the 'divinities of my father', for the sick
man 'is the child of your daughter, and if you abandon him to
death, then all the Powers will mock at you. And if you let him live,
then you have helped the child of your daughter'. The officiant goes
on to call upon his departed parents and grandparents, 'that you
may help me when I pray about sickness, the sickness of my sister's
child. My sister's child shall be well. . . . If I call upon you, then
you will agree (accept my prayer).' He tells them, as he has told God
and the divinities, that he has 'stayed in peace with them', and has
no malice against the sick man. His prayer is being made in the
purity of the heart. Therefore it deserves acceptance by God, the
divinities and the living dead.

At the end of such a pure and heart-searching prayer, one would
only say, 'Amen: let it be so!' It has used high-powered reasoning
and argument to support its central wish: that the sick man should
be healed and not left to die. The power of healing is in the hands
of spiritual realities, including God himself, the divinities and the
living dead. Man takes a firm stand in the issue, and simply or
notoriously tells the spiritual powers, 'we have refused death this
day'. He argues his case with serious and convincing reasons.

These, then, are some of the prayers for life and healing which
African peoples offer to God, the spirits and the living dead. Sometimes the appeal is clearly made to God alone; sometimes, to the
spirits alone; sometimes, only to the living dead; and often, to two
or all three of these spiritual realities. When making such prayers,
man is more interested in receiving help than in sorting out from
whom or where it may have come. He appeals to the spiritual
realities as a totality, having given up the possibility of getting help
from the physical realm of this life.

It is remarkable how African peoples so confidently address spiritual realities. In many of their prayers for healing, there is virtually no barrier between the realm of man and the spiritual realm. Man argues with these realities as if he saw them face to face. Man even politely rebukes them as if they had become unreasonable. (In ch. 6, prayer 120 presents a man so angry with God over a child's death that he threatens to kill him if he finds him!) This is an outstanding dimension of African spirituality, and it should not be carelessly judged simply as spirit or ancestor worship, by people who only betray their ignorance about African religious feeling and practice. Praying is not all worship: it is also rhetorical dialogue, a one-way dialogue, a platform for man's questioning and heart-searching, in the presence of God and the other spiritual realities.

PRAYERS FOR LIFE

23 Prayer for clinging to life[1]

We have come to thee, O Do [God], to ask for life. Help us to cling to it. Thou well knowest that the person who has slain a poisoner must make haste. We know thou art a strong God, and have faith in thee. Hasten to help us cling to life, and those whom thou hast protected will gather sea shells for thee and buy a goat to offer up to thee. Here is the water we pour out to thee with one hand, and thou acceptest it with two hands.

24 For life to my people[2]

The edges of the years have met, I take sheep and new yams and
    give you that you may eat.
Life to me.
Life to this my Ashanti people.
Women who cultivate the farms, when they do so, grant that the
    food comes forth in abundance.
Do not allow any illness to come.

25 To the living dead who once shared this life[3]

O good and innocent dead, hear us: hear us, you guiding, all-knowing ancestors, you are neither blind nor deaf to this life we live: you did yourselves once share it. Help us therefore for the sake of our devotion, and for our good.

26 Let life multiply[4]

O Death, you who domicile with a person and imbue him with
nobility!
O Sceptre-Wielder!
O you who multiply one into two hundred persons!
Multiply me into four hundred,
Multiply me into two hundred,
Multiply me into one thousand four hundred and sixty persons.

PRAYERS FOR HEALTH AND HEALING

27 For a sick child[5]

O God, thou art great,
Thou art the One who created me,
I have no other.
God, thou art in the heavens,
Thou art the only One:
Now my child is sick,
And thou wilt grant me my desire.

28 For help in sickness[6]

You, Father God,
Who are in the heavens and below;
Creator of everything and omniscient;
Of the earth and the heavens;
We are but little children
Unknowing anything evil;
If this sickness has been brought by man
We beseech you, help us through these roots.
In case it was inflicted by you, the Conserver,
Likewise do we entreat your mercy on your child;
Also you, our grandparents, who sleep in the place of the shades,
We entreat all of you who sleep on one side.
All ancestors, males and females, great and small,
Help us in this trouble, have compassion on us;
So that we can also sleep peacefully.
And thus do I spit out this mouthful of water!
Pu-pu! Pu-pu!
Please listen to our earnest request.

29 For a wife's recovery[7]

Thou alone, O God, hast ordained that we marry women. Therefore grant that my wife, now sick, recover speedily.

30 For recovery[8]

O great Deng [God], let her live,
Let her recover and escape from death,
O great Deng, let her live!

31 Prayer of blessing for the sick[9]

LEADER: PEOPLE:

(a young person of good character)   *(utter agreement)*

Akongo [God] of the ancestors,   mokanga
Akongo of my fathers,   mokanga
Akongo of the fathers,   mokanga
I broke no commandment of yours,
I chopped firewood in the rain,
When I killed (an animal) I hid nothing.
So-and-so is suffering,
Make his body strong,
Let him, Akongo.
I leave off.
(spits) Bless, Kunda, bless.

32 Prayer of a medicine-man when treating the sick[10]

We pray and we say:

God help this man that he may be well;
    that he may recover tomorrow,
And may you want to help this man to be well,
    and as overcoming you overcame,
Overcome all these troubles.
And have mercy on me,
    because we do not know how to pray to Murungu [God]
    differently from what we say now.

33 For recovery from spirit sickness[11]

See, if you have made this child sick;
See the goat you always receive;
See, I have lighted a fire for you;
See your child;

Let him be healed so that he may care for your things;
Let our home be peaceful.

34 Prayer in a serious sickness[12]

If you are such and such spirits [*emandwa ezeera*, or *ezirangura*, or
    ezobukuratire],
Release this child;
See, I have lighted a fire for you.
See, I have given you beer and food.
Eat and be content.
Meanwhile, the child will prepare himself.
He will be initiated;
And he will give worship and offerings to you.
For now, if you do not heal him,
Who will prepare the feast,
The feast of initiation for you?
Let him go free, spare him.
He is going to work for your feast;
He knows that you are making a demand of him.
He will fulfil your demand;
And you will be satisfied.

35 Soliciting help in an influenza epidemic[13]

Let the great ones gather!
What have we done to suffer so?
We do not say, Let so-and-so come, we say, all!
Here your children are in distress.
There is not one able to give a drink of water to another.
Wherein have we erred?
Here is food, we give to you;
Aid us, your children.

36 Where is the promise?[14]

The promise that you promised, you of my father, where is it? You
trees, hear my words; and you grass, hear my words; and you
Divinity, hear my words and you earth, hear my words. Repeat, ee!
O Divinity, because of sickness, you will help out my tongue. For
we have dedicated the ox and invoked over it. And if a man has
hated Akol (and his sickness is the result of malice) then that man
will find what he deserves.

37 Another man continues with the previous prayer:

Repeat, ee! A person whom I shall spy out I will knot up in grass,
and you Akol will get up. And you ox we have given you to the
illness. And you fetish-bundles, thay say that you kill people. Leave
off, you are shamed [frightened]. You fetish I have separated you,
cease! And you Macardit they say that you kill people: I have
separated you, cease! Thus! My words are finished. You of my
father, I have called you to help me; and you of my mother, I have
called you to help me.

38 For sending sickness into the bush[15]

*In front of a sick man's house where a black chicken, and other things,
are placed on the ground:*

I draw you right out, a,a, right out into the bush.
I lay a spell on you with my *ogudo*, with my thorn tree,
With my *kigelia*, with my chicken.
I take you right away; leave the body of my embryo (child)
    that it may be well.
I cast a spell on you with the spear
    with which our ancestors formerly cast spells on sickness,
    a,a, you come right out.

39 Invocations over plague patients[16]

I sing then, Omarari,
I sing then, Omarari,
Omarari, let thy wrath cease.
I sing then, Omarari,
I sing then, Omarari,
Omarari, let thy wrath cease.
Children who are, are the children of Omarari:
Let thy wrath cease.
Lads who are, are the lads of Omarari:
Let thy wrath cease.
Girls that are, are the girls of Omarari:
Let thy wrath cease.
I sing then, to Omarari,
Omarari, let thy wrath cease.

A, A, what is that cry which they cry at Achaba?
I cry Omarari.
A, A, what is that cry which they cry at Aber?
I cry Omarari.

A, A, what is that cry which they cry among the Acholi?
I cry Omarari.
A, A, this cry which they cry they cry, the chiefs, e, e,
A, A, this road which they make they make, the chiefs, e, e.

40 Sacrificial prayers for recovery from sickness[17]

Before the sacrificial sheep for a sick man, this is repeated:

LEADER: *Ogwal*	OLD MEN:
Let this sickness forget	Forget
If it goes, good	Good
If the village is at rest, good	Good
May the dead forget	Forget

(*continued in* 41)

41 *While dragging the sheep into the bush:*

LEADER:	OLD MEN:
If you are Atim, if you are Ongu	
(*dead wives of the sick man*),	
Let the people of the dead forget	Let the people of the dead forget
If the village is at rest, good	Good
May the sickness forget.	Forget.

42 Appeal to the spirits to help the sick[18]

First Plea

O thou Gumede!
O thou Mputa!
Here is your beast.
That your child may be healed,
Look on what is yours.
May you remain well
And your children recover.
We do not know,
We do not know
If you say that she will die,
She is yours, this child of yours.
It is your affair;
As for us, we long that your child may recover.
If she dies, this child of yours,
We can only speak your names;
We cry to you for help.

43 *Second Plea*

Alas, O Paramount,
Alas, O Father,
Why do you refuse us?
What do you say about your child?
We say we are your people,
Alas, O Paramount.

44 Pleading with the departed for a child's recovery[19]

At the cattle enclosure

Yes, grandfathers Pato and Kuzi [*grandfather and great grandfather of the child*], you were asking. Today we give you this beast that you may eat, and the child may be well.

45 *Repeat the plea*

Here is your beast, Manywana of Mijola, Linganiso. We are making well he who is ill. We wish peace between us.

Here is your beast, here is the thing you wish [people] of Kiwo, Ntskinyane, Nogemane, and Gwadiso.

46 Offertory prayer of a sick man[20]

What is it, chiefs? I want to be well. Here then, is the thing I am giving you.

47 Litany for a sick child[21]

MOTHER: O spirits of the past, this little one I hold is my child: she is your child also, therefore, be gracious unto her.

WOMEN, *chanting*: She has come into a world of trouble: sickness is in the world, and cold and pain: the pain you knew: the sickness with which you were familiar.

MOTHER: Let her sleep in peace, for there is healing in sleep: let none among you be angry with me or with my child.

WOMEN: Let her grow: let her become strong: let her become full-grown: then will she offer such a sacrifice to you that will delight your hearts.

48 Litany for a sick man[22]

WIFE: O spirits of my husband; his fathers of the long ago: let thy breath be cool upon his brow.

RELATIVES: We pray you, O friendly ones: gain for this our sick one the goodwill of those that bless and heal.

49 'We have refused death this day'[23]

O you earth, and you divinity of my father, we have refused death this day. And you Nhialic [God], we have refused death this day. You fetish, a man buys you for a cow and you come in order to help him. If a man goes to a distant country and possesses a fetish he travels in health, and if a man goes to collect cattle which are owed to him, you walk with him. For if a man finds evil in the path, he will call you, saying: 'Come let me be in health.' And you ox, it is not for nothing that we have tethered you in the midday sun, but because of sickness, to exchange your life for the man, and for the man to stay on earth and for your life to go with the illness. You Nhialic hear my speech, and you clan-divinity hear my speech, and you illness I have separated you from the man. I have spoken thus: 'You leave the man alone, you have been given the ox called *malith*.' Thus! You child of my sister, repeat my words!

I am not a man from another tribe, I am a man of this land in the tribe of Apuk Jurwir here. I am not a bastard coming with its mother, the bastard fathered by some stranger outside. If such a one prays, he calls upon no clan-divinity, because he is a child which comes with his mother alone and he will be unable to do anything in a case of sickness. Nhialic is within the man who has him. The earth is spoilt by this illness. Flesh of my father, come forth! Wuu, away the sickness!

Here those present make the sound 'wuu' loudly and move their heads and arms in the direction of the non-Dinka peoples to the south, sending the illness there. Then the concluding invocation follows:

You, Nhialic [God], I do not want words of such sickness, that a man should be ill. O you of my father, do not let me speak a lie! And you Nhialic I have called upon you because Akol Agany had no sister born with him, and you of my father, Akol Agany has been very unfortunate [miserable, poor, unlucky] in Apuk, the tribe of his father.

Why is it, O Nhialic, that when one son is left alive alone out of all the children his mother bore, you do not help him, that he may be in health? You Nhialic, if you have left Akol Agany behind to beget children, and he now becomes ill, we have refused [to accept] this illness in him.

For Akol Agany has no sister born with him, and no brother born with him, and if Nhialic does not help him to bear his children, then the children will become the children of the mother [*i.e. his line will die out*]. And you Nhialic you are the great person, father of all people, and if a man has called upon you you will strengthen his arm, that no evil may befall him.

And you Agany senior [the dead father of the sick man] why have you left your child in misery in his father's tribe? In the past, when you were alive, you left Akol as an only child, with no sister and brother, and he himself begot his own brother and sister [*i.e. he begot children from a wife of his deceased father*].

It is you divinities of my father that I call upon to come and help the child Akol Agany, that he may live. He is the child of your daughter, and if you abandon him to death, then all the Powers will mock at you [despise you]. And if you let him live, then you have helped the child of your daughter. And you of my father, I did not neglect you [treat you lightly] on the occasion in the past when my father died, it is not so, it is not true that I caused confusion in the descent group of my father.

You my own father, and you my grandfather and you my grandmother and you my mother, I have called upon you that you may help me when I pray about sickness, the sickness of my sister's child. My sister's child shall be well. I did not quarrel with the family of your daughter, I stayed in peace with them, and I meant no malice against my sister's children. If I call upon you, then will you agree [to accept my prayer].

4 *For wealth and prosperity*

The prayers available to me on the theme of wealth all refer to cattle, sheep and goats. In the majority of African societies one or more of these domestic animals constitutes the centre of personal or family wealth. The animals are utilized in such various ways as the provision of food and milk, the exchange of goods, social entertainment, sacrifices, and marriage arrangements. The prayers for livestock indicate how much these animals are valued. Many of the traditional raids are still carried out for the capture or recapture of cattle, sheep and goats. Many people today who earn money spend it on buying cattle. In some societies the life of the cattle is valued above that of people.

Prayers 50 and 51 are short invocations of joy and delight at the arrival of raided cattle. The Nandi, like the Masai, are well known for their raiding skills. These raided cattle are interpreted (50) as a sign of good health and prosperity from God. Prayer 52 is a one line invocation which accompanies the anointing of sheep after disease has broken out. The next invocation is also for the good health of sheep; and 54 is a prayer before cattle lick salt lest they be poisoned or otherwise harmed.

The invocations 55, 56 and 57 request God to give people wealth as cattle, sheep, goats and children. People include their children in the same category as cattle to indicate the great value that they attach to livestock on which so much of their life depends. In their view, it is useless to have children without cattle, sheep or goats, for without such wealth the children would starve and be unable to marry. Likewise a wealth of livestock without children in a family is useless. Animal wealth is an insurance against starvation, hunger, poverty, and the unmarried life. For that reason, people pray to be given both animals and children which together constitute a balanced prosperity for a family.

Victory in war is one of the vanities of mankind. Here we have two examples of victory prayers. The first (58) is a solemn chant of praise for victory. In it Tomukujen (God) is acknowledged to be the maker of mankind, to order people's goings, and to have guided this group of warriors into victory. The victorious raiders laugh in self-satisfaction: 'Our enemies are scattered. It is well.' Then in a

vivid and beautiful manner they describe how 'we have winnowed
them (enemies) as the chaff falls from the basket . . . as the chaff
they fall and are silent'. The enemies have fallen like ashes, they are
scattered, but for the victor 'it is well'. They recall how their spears
knocked down the young men on the enemy's side, how wives were
widowed, daughters made fatherless and cattle driven away. The
homesteads of the enemy are empty, without lowing of cattle, even
suffering a shortage of dung for the fires. Then in a new stanza the
victory song continues afresh, greeting God and the spirits: 'Ha:
Tomukujen, we greet Thee. Spirits of our fathers, we greet you.'
This is a moment of great rejoicing, therefore greetings are sent to
God and the living dead, in order that they, too, may share in the
jubilation of victory. The prayer-song goes on to mention where the
battle was fought and against whom the victory was won. The
Didinga, who recite this prayer, still raid the Dodoth and the
Turkana, whom they mention here as having been defeated.

In the final stanza the prayer moves away from the note of pride
and self-gratification to one of humility. The warriors do not want
it to sound as if they have won the victory entirely in their own
strength. So they ask their forefathers to 'help us . . . (and) guard
us, our fathers, and it is well'. They also pray that the spirits of the
dead enemies will be quiet and trouble them no more. There is
a common fear among some African peoples that cruel death may
cause the spirit of the victim to return and take revenge on those
who killed him. So here the warriors do not want to face an attack
more fierce from the spirits of those already defeated in physical
battle. They pray, therefore, that these spirits 'be bewildered and find
us not . . . seeking hither and thither witless like one lost in a forest'.

This is a magnificent prayer-song of victory, with a vivid account
of what happened in battle, acknowledging that victory was won
through God's help and asking in humility that the warriors be
guarded and protected from harassment by the spirits of their
enemies.

The second victory prayer (59) is very brief but it nevertheless
puts across the joy and shouts of jubilation. Both God and Lenana,
a ritual expert, are thought responsible for the victory. Presumably
this prayer was popular among the followers of Lenana, who came
to power in 1890. The prayer acknowledges divine and human
help in the victory won by the cattle-raiding warriors. The song is
sung while the warriors drive off the cattle to their own homesteads.
The medicine-man is undoubtedly the one consulted before the

raid is undertaken to advise whether or not it should take place.

Hunting has been, from time immemorial, one of the main occupations of African peoples. In prayer 60 the hunter makes a straightforward request: 'Give me game, make me find honey and roots.' He is deeply concerned because his welfare depends on finding them. They constitute the essential food necessary for himself and his family; and failure to obtain them means hunger and starvation for him and his people. His finding game is dependent upon help from God who is the father and grandfather of the people. When the hunter succeeds he will again bless or thank God through whom he has obtained his happiness and prosperity which are the most valued possessions in life. Therefore game and foodstuffs feature prominently in his prayer!

Prayer 61 for prosperity is offered by the *mugwe*, the ritual leader of the Meru people. It addresses God as the 'owner of all things', and the *mugwe* informs him that everyone is suffering in Meru country. So he begs for life, riches, health, children, fertility of women, cattle and food. The *mugwe* is very sensitive to the needs of his people, being specially concerned about the 'women who suffer because they are barren' and for whom he asks that God may 'open fully the way, by which they may see children'. The *mugwe* extends his concern beyond tribal boundaries, and asks for universal prosperity as he prays that God will remove 'also the troubles of the other lands I do not know'. This note of universal outlook is rare in the prayers of this collection.

Prayer 62 asks for prosperity from the departed grandfathers 'who completed so many noble undertakings'. It opens with a note of diplomatic praise for the departed, in keeping with common practice of 'praising' those in authority before one asks favour of them. The man has sacrificed a bull to the living dead, it is now theirs; so he is entitled to ask them for 'every kind of prosperity'.

He names his priorities: 'many beasts to fill these tables! . . . much grain . . . (and) numerous offspring', not for his selfish acquisition but for his community at large. He foresees the impact of this prosperity because he hopes that productive lands will attract more people to settle there who then would 'make much tumult to your (living dead's) glory'; and that the numerous offspring would ensure that 'your names may never be extinguished'. This type of prosperity is, in effect, to be returned to the departed: it is for their welfare and happiness. The physical blessings sought from the world of the spirits are to be translated into spiritual blessings which in turn are sent back to the spiritual world. Thus, if the departed grant herds of animals, plentiful harvests and innumerable children to the people, the people will honour the departed and their names will be remembered indefinitely. This is a comprehensive form of prosperity which embraces both the living and the departed, men and spirits.

Three prayers for protection are included here, all of which are short and simple. In prayer 63, God is asked to protect the homestead from all possible dangers. The man who is praying is not sure whether or not to sacrifice a cow in order to propitiate God. He asks God, nevertheless, as Father and metaphorically husband (of both women and cows), to exercise his protective care over the home. The imagery of father and husband reinforces God's protective position which is higher or more powerful than that of the human father and husband. Prayer 64 is an invocation made by the head of the family, asking God to guard the children and cattle for him and other people, and to give them health. Although it is very short, this invocation shows us the things that the man values most in his life: children, cattle and health. We have already seen prayers for the increase or prosperity of cattle offered by the Nandi and other peoples (50 and following). It is only consistent, therefore, that those who value cattle so much should pray for their protection and welfare. Prayer 65 is for personal protection against snake-bite. Quite understandably, it is addressed to the arch-snake of the people, presumably their totemic animal and hence the symbol of their welfare. In this request, both people and other snakes are the sons and children of this tribal snake. Because there are so many snakes in Africa, and because people have so general a fear of them, it is no wonder that such a prayer should have been created.

In the prayers for wealth, success and prosperity, African peoples indicate their conviction that man's physical welfare ultimately depends upon the spiritual realm of God and the departed. Man has to solicit spiritual help to make his physical life harmonize with the spiritual realities surrounding him. Human abilities are limited, and at this point of their finitude, God, the spiritual realm, and the living dead take over. Yet these two realms are not mutually exclusive: man must do his part as far as he can, while at the same time seeking assistance from the divine or spiritual side. People are not hesitant to ask for physical riches and prosperity, which in a sense become a measure of favour or blessings from God and the departed where applicable. It is to be noted that they also share their prosperity with God and the departed, through sacrifices, thanksgiving, and other acts of remembrance.

PRAYERS FOR CATTLE AND WEALTH

50 For integrating raided cattle[1]

The raided cattle, oh!
The raided cattle, oh!
The raided cattle, oh!
God, he has given us health!

51 To welcome raided cattle into the fenced homestead[2]

The cattle, my! come into this house which is warm.
And do not ye say: 'We are few.'
Ye come slowly and ye stay quietly.

52 When anointing sheep[3]

God! give us the belly which is good.

53 For protection of sheep[4]

Before the gathering that feasted on the sheep separates, the following prayer is recited by all:

God! have-we-prayed-thee,
Cover for us these here.

54 Invocation if cattle are poisoned[5]

God make good for us the salt lick.
If any ox eats the salt, may it like it.

55 For increase of cattle[6]

God, we are hungry,
Give us cattle, give us sheep!

At their sacrifices, the officiating elder prays:

God, increase cattle,
Increase sheep, increase men!

56 For obtaining sheep and children[7]

O God my Father, give me goats,
Give me sheep, give me children,
That I may be rich, O God my Father.

57 Litany for goats and children[8]

MUGWE INVOKES: PEOPLE RESPOND:

Let us pray God: Pray,
   for goats: Pray,
   for cattle: Pray,
   for children: Pray,
Let us pray God: Pray.

VICTORY AND SUCCESS

58 Praise for victory[9]

Tomukujen [God], who madest us,
Tomukujen who didst order our goings,
Tomukujen who didst guide our spears:
Behold us return victorious,
Our enemies are scattered. It is well.

We have winnowed them as the chaff which falls from the basket.
As the chaff is carried by the wind are they driven this way and
   that.
As the chaff they fall and are silent.
Like ashes thrown out on the midden when in the morning the house
   is swept by the women.
They fall *pum* like ashes thrown on a midden.
We are returned victorious.
Our enemies are scattered. It is well.
There are tears and lamentation in their villages;
There is lamentation for their young men that are dead,
For their young men whom our spears caused to stumble.
Their wives are widowed and their daughters are fatherless.
There is sorrow for the cattle which our warriors have driven away;
There is sorrow for the empty homestead, for the cattlesheds that
   are silent, wherein is no lowing of oxen, and the dung fires burn
   low and are extinguished.
Ho for the captives!
The women who shall be as our women, the fair maidens meet for
   motherhood!
Swelling hips and breasts like melons!
Ha! Tomukujen, we greet thee.
Spirits of our fathers, we greet you.

By the great fight which we fought at Naita when the Turkana were driven back, we adjure you.

By the Black Bull which was tied at Chebchya, we adjure you.

By the memory of Lomalir where we laid waste the villages of Dodoth, we adjure you.

We have winnowed them as the chaff which falls from the basket and they are dead.

They lie in great heaps.

Help us, our fathers, and it is well.

Guard us, our fathers, and it is well.

May their spirits be at peace, may they trouble us not nor be disquieted.

May they be bewildered, seeking hither and thither,

Witless like one lost in a forest.

Ha, Tomukujen, our enemies are scattered.

Their villages are desolate and the death cry is caught from house to house, from river to river.

59 A litany of victory[10]

LEADER: CHORUS RESPONSE:

I pray that this may be my year,   Wo-ho! Woo-hoo!
It is to God that I pray.   Wo-ho! Woo-hoo!

I pray that this may be my year,   Wo-ho! Woo-hoo!
It is to Lenana that I pray.   Wo-ho! Woo-hoo!

Our medicine-man, our medicine-man,
We tell you: Wo-ho! Woo-hoo!
The homesteads are full of bullocks.   Wo-ho! Woo-hoo!

60 For a successful hunt[11]

O Heitsi-eibib [God?]!
Thou, our grandfather,
Grant me happiness!
Give me game,
Make me find honey and roots,
That I may bless thee again!
O Heitsi-eibib,
Art thou not our grandfather?

PROSPERITY AND PROTECTION

61 Invocation for national prosperity[12]

God, owner of all things,
I pray thee, give me what I need
    because I am suffering,
And also my children [are suffering] and all the things that are in
    this country of mine.
I beg thee for life, the good one with things [rich life];
Healthy people with no disease,
May they bear healthy children;
And also to women who suffer because they are barren,
Open fully the way by which they may see children.
Give goats, cattle, food, honey;
And also the troubles of the other lands that I do not know,
Remove.

62 For many kinds of prosperity[13]

Yes! Yes! I implore you, O grandfathers who completed so many
noble undertakings! Having sacrificed this bull which belongs to
you, I pray to you, asking of you every kind of prosperity. I cannot
deny you nourishment, since you have given me all the herds that
are here, and if you ask of me the nourishment that you have given
me, is it not just that I return it to you? Grant us many beasts to
fill these tables! Grant us much grain, so that many people may
come to inhabit this village which is yours and so may make much
tumult to your glory. Grant us numerous offspring, so that this
village may be much populated and your names may never be
extinguished!

63 For protection of the home[14]

You Divinity [God], protect the homestead.
Shall I not propitiate you with a cow?
Divinity, Father, you protect the home.
Husband of the cows,
Husband of the women,
It is you who protect the home.

64 'God, guard for me . . .'[15]

God, guard for me the children and cattle,

God, guard for us the cattle,
God, give us health!

65 Protection against snake bite[16]

When the foot in the night
Stumbles against the obstacle that shrinks and rears and bites,
Let, O Snake, thou our Father, Father of our tribe,
We are thy sons,
Let it be a branch that rears and strikes,
But not one of thy sharp-toothed children,
O Father of the tribe, we are thy sons.

5 *For man's work*

The prayers grouped in this chapter are those which deal with people's livelihood, particularly farming, healing, hunting and travelling. Food and health are universal and fundamental concerns of mankind throughout the world. The prayers presented here reveal something of African preoccupations with these concerns, and the forms of spirituality which have evolved out of them.

The agricultural year begins with sowing and ends with harvesting. Prayers 66–75 give us a cross-section of ideas and concerns for the agricultural year. Prayer 66 is a dedication of seeds and farming implements before sowing. People acknowledge that they are God's creatures. They tell him that they have no strength. In humility they ask him to bless their seeds, implements and themselves, in order to 'make good use of them by the power which comes from you, our Creator'. This is a prayer of deep humility in which man presents himself as being entirely dependent upon God who has 'all power'. It is hard to work in the fields, using hoes, sticks or simple ploughs, throughout the year, and such hard work will be rewarded only if there is enough rain. As the rain comes only from God, people have to ask him for an abundant supply. (Cf. ch. 9.)

Prayer 67 opens beautifully with greetings to God and the living dead! It is an important social convention in African societies to greet other people before presenting one's business. The prayer is offered on a 'chosen day: we are going to sow the seed'. The people ask God to cause their crops to grow and bear abundantly. It is also a prayer for women to conceive, and for protection against thorns, snake bites, and dangerous winds, as people go about their work. All the labour of sowing, cultivating and working in the fields depends on rain. Therefore God is besought to 'pour out the rain, as we pour water from the pot!' Abundance of rain will mean abundance of grain. This prayer conveys and summarizes the aspirations of many African peoples.

Prayer 68 is dynamic, powerful and vivid. It summons the earth to be kind, fertile and generous to the people who dig, sow and work on it. 'Be fertile when they give little seeds to your keeping' is a beautiful expression of man's wish to be in absolute harmony with the earth on which he depends for his livelihood. If the earth shows its care, the people will soon 'redden your bosom with the blood of goats slain in your honour, and offer you the first fruits of your munificence . . .' in a great act of thanksgiving.

The second stanza addresses the trees that have to be cut down to prepare the fields. 'Be gentle to my people. Let no harm come to them. Break no limb in your anger. Crush no one in your displeasure.' All these are requests for safety, so that people can clear the forests without danger to their lives: 'Fall, O trees of forest and glade . . . hurting no one.'

In the third paragraph, the prayer summons rivers and streams so that they may water the ground to be used as fields. They are asked to deposit their fertile humus and silt on the fields: 'Spread out your waters and lay your rich treasures on our gardens.'

In conclusion the prayer calls upon the earth, forest and rivers to 'conspire together, O earth and rivers and forests. Be gentle and give us plenty from your teeming plenty.' The prayer is offered by the 'Keeper of the clan lands, Warden of the Forest, Master of the clan'. It is a fully authorized prayer, carrying the full weight of traditional, official, political, and religious authority. It is addressed to the earth, the forests and rivers, as though these were intelligent realities. Man treats nature here as personal and intelligent; he personifies it in order to be able to communicate with it, solicit its help and even order it about for his own welfare. At the same time man seems to realize that earth, forests and rivers do not necessarily follow his commands blindly; therefore he has to plead with them, and wait on their favour. Man has also to express his gratitude at least to the earth by offering first fruits and the blood of goats. All these sentiments show man's wish to have a harmonious relationship with nature, without treating nature exclusively as a utility. If man abuses nature, nature will, in return, abuse him.

A sacrifice is made to the 'earth of my clan', in order to solicit its kindness, in prayer 69. Evidently a man who is a newcomer or stranger to an area intends to cultivate a field. But he cannot do that without regard to the earth. Therefore a ritual is performed in order to bring the newcomer into harmony with the soil where he intends to establish his field. For this, an indigenous dweller must act as the intermediary, and introduce him: 'Deal kindly with Lokuryamoi, for he is our friend . . . grant him a harvest as rich as our own.' This prayer integrates the stranger into the local community, the soil and birds and beasts of that area. The stranger is put into harmony with nature, before he can settle down. This, too, is a moving prayer for man's harmony with nature. African peoples have a mystical relationship with the land, and these two prayers are a clear illustration of that relationship.

Praise and thanksgiving at harvest time are the themes of prayers 70 and 71. (There are other prayers of praise and thanksgiving in chapter 12.) God is asked to 'let people eat grain of this harvest calmly and peacefully', and to guard them and their herds 'so that we may enjoy this season's harvest in tranquillity'. Having worked hard they want to enjoy the fruit of their labours in peace. The short invocation given in 71 accompanies an act of thank-offering to God, in form of bread made from the first harvest of the millet crop. This bread is offered at the family shrine, and both God and the spirits are invited to partake of it. In the invocation God is acknowledged as the all-seeing, ever watchful Kazooba (Sun), the Creator and Giver of all things. Man only returns gratefully a small portion of what God has given to him in plenty.

Prayers 72, 73 and 74 are offered at harvest time. In prayer 72 a hyperbole figure of speech is employed to demonstrate the abundance of the harvest which would cover the pathways and fields with grain. In 73 people wish to receive good health from God, so that they may enjoy their abundant milk. Milk is one of the chief foods of the Nandi and a number of other pastoral and agricultural peoples. Here it symbolizes the abundance of food. The next invocation (74) comes also from the Nandi people, and is offered at harvest time by the elders. They ask for health, cattle and children, which constitute three fundamental elements of man's needs according to many African peoples. The final invocation included in this group of harvest prayers (75) is one in which the head of the family brews beer, offers it to the spirits and invites them to share a meal of the first fruits of the harvest. It is recited under the same circumstances as 71. Many African people feel the presence of their dead relatives as part of their surviving families. It is an act of respect and remembrance to invite them to share, at least symbolically, in a meal or new harvest. By offering the first fruits, man has symbolically offered the entire crop to God (or the living dead), and is now able to eat it without feeling a sense of meanness towards the spiritual realm.

The first prayer for the work of the medicine-man or diviner (76) is from Ashanti priests and is used by someone who does the work of both priest and diviner. It is addressed to the spiritual population: God, divinities and the living dead, inviting them all to accept a

libation of wine. 'Come, all of you, and accept this wine and drink.
Stand behind me with a good standing . . .' They are to support
him in his work, so that 'If any is sick, let me able to tend him.' He
asks that he may also divine and say good things to the chief since
saying unpleasant truths can be dangerous for any diviner. Many
traditional kings and chiefs in African societies (as well as
reportedly some modern presidents and other political leaders) have
diviners whom they consult about their fortunes and undertakings.
It is well known that when the diviners predict or reveal things
which are contrary to the expectations of the rulers and leaders, they
often fall into disfavour. Sometimes such leaders even threaten the
diviners and warn them against divining bad things. It is for these
reasons that this particular prayer asks that what the diviner has to
tell the king (chief) should be acceptable and good. He also prays to
be protected against impotence, against blindness and against
deafness, which mean a premature end to his work. The final
request has a moral concern: 'Do not let my penis make a slave of my
neck.' The diviner and priest are people of great moral integrity,
and their work would be ruined by uncontrolled sexual enslavement.
This prayer asks help from God and the spiritual realm, for self-
control.

Prayer 77 strikes a mystical note which is rare in African prayers.
The medicine-man addresses God (Spirit) as being able to do all
things, without whom 'I am powerless, I am powerless'. He tells
God that he is 'consecrated to thee, I who am pledged to thee'. It is
difficult to interpret the meaning of 'consecrated to thee'. It may be
that the medicine-man has taken a ritual promise, vow or covenant to
serve in his profession. It may also mean that the man was dedicated
as a child by his parents to be a medicine-man. In any case he is
entirely dependent upon God, and gets his strength or skill from
him. 'Thou brought me the gift' may mean that he acknowledges
his gift of healing work to have come from God. The medicine-man
then invites the Spirit to 'come, come', since he has given him what
he wanted, a sacrifice placed in the forest. The man ends his prayer
with a mystical acknowledgment: 'Spirit, I am thine, thou art
mine, come to me!' This prayer has several elements that echo
passages or concepts in the Gospel of St John, such as 'without thee
I am powerless' (cf. John 15.5, 'without me you can do nothing'),
'consecrated to thee' (cf. John 17.19, 'I consecrate myself, that they
also may be consecrated in truth'), the use of 'Spirit' (cf. John 16),
'I am thine, thou art mine' (cf. John 17.10, 'all mine are thine, and

thine are mine'), and the notion of coming which is also common in St John's Gospel. One has no background information to this prayer, which would help in establishing whether or not Christian influence has played a role in its construction.

The next prayer (78) is offered by a medicine-man in order that his work may be effective: 'Jouk (God) my Father, help us heal this (so and so).' It is a prayer of humbleness; the man confesses that he has a clean moral life, has stolen nothing and has 'no sin' in his soul. He sacrifices a ram, and pleads that God should take the ram and 'leave us the child, grant that he recover'.

This idea of sacrificing an animal during a healing ceremony is also represented in other prayers. An animal life, is, as it were, destroyed so that human life may be spared, 'redeemed'. The medicine-man is conscious of moral purity, as in prayer 76. He does not confess his wickedness: he declares before God that he is morally upright, and on those grounds he seeks a positive answer to his prayer.

The brief invocation for effective medicine (79) talks about the saliva. We have previously pointed out that the saliva is used by African peoples in the act of blessing. This prayer would mean, therefore, that the medicine-man has no personal source of blessing (healing) people and depends entirely on God 'the possessor of saliva' (blessings). Therefore he asks God to 'spit upon' (bless) his medicine in order to make it effective. The next two invocations, 80 and 81, ask for blessings upon medicinal herbs and their use, so that they may effect the cure for which they are applied.

Invocations 82 and 83 are recited in a divination setting. They are to produce the knowledge of what has happened (whether or not a man has slept with his wives), or what will happen in an undertaking.

Six prayers are included, concerning mining, hunting and fishing. The prayer in search of iron ore (84) is brief. It asks God for health and iron wealth. Before undertaking a hunting expedition, a hunter consults the oracle in prayer 85, to find out whether it will succeed or be frustrated by witchcraft. But in prayer 86, a group of hunters approaches God directly, with the request: 'Our God: we have come to your place, Give us animals: many animals, Lest we go back with shame.' They perform a ritual around a tree appropriately called *Edatito* ('there will be animals'). It would be a great shame and disappointment for them to return home empty-handed as the women would laugh at them and the living dead would be displeased. Even before they kill any animals, this prayer gives them enough

confidence to speak as though they had succeeded already, to anticipate the joy they and their wives will experience. 'We rejoice . . . they (the women) are also glad.' And this confidence is sealed with the belief that their forefathers and the God of their fathers have agreed to give them many animals in the hunt. This is a clear illustration of prayers which combine a request and at the same time the anticipated receipt of what is requested. Time is bridged by a simple but sincere faith which allows virtually no room for a request to be rejected or unfulfilled.

Prayer 87 is in two parts, one of which puts out the urgent request of the hunters, 'Let us kill today before sunset.' The other part declares the joyful gratitude they express to God after their success: 'I thank thee for the meat which thou givest me.' The second part is like the harvest thanksgiving prayers which we have already discussed.

Only two prayers (88 and 89) are printed here relating to the work of fishermen. The first, brief thought it is, summarizes the concerns of the fisherman on duty: 'a calm lake, little wind, little rain, so that the canoes may proceed well'. The fisherman does not waste words: he knows what he needs, and he presents it all in one sentence to God. The second fisherman's prayer (89) is also straightforward and reasonably brief. It is addressed to the river or presumably the spirit of the river as a personification: 'O river, I beg leave to take fish from thee, as my ancestors did before me.' This is another example of man wanting to be in harmony with nature: rivers, water, crocodiles, and fish, as in the case of sowing and working in the fields (67, 68 and 69). Nature's riches are not to be exploited carelessly or lightly: man treats nature as he would treat a friend, with respect. In this prayer, man is asking to fish in peace and free from danger: 'O river, rise up, engulf your sharp-toothed monsters, and permit our young men to enter the water and enjoy themselves with the fish without being harmed.' In token of this request, the fisherman offers a baby chick; and if the river cannot sufficiently control the 'sharp-toothed monsters' (crocodiles and hippopotami), then it should indicate so by rejecting the offering. This offering constitutes a simple form of divination, and the prayer is presumably recited by a local priest, diviner, or medicine-man. The prayer belongs to a group of similar ceremonial prayers recited at sowing and harvesting times.

There are only two prayers for travelling. Prayer 90 is like an incantation addressed probably to a sacred stone, to 'retard the sun on high so that I can arrive first'. The traveller is going on foot, and while he is still a long way off, the sun nears setting time. He knows that darkness will soon fall, and he will probably lose his way or have to reckon with unseen dangers. He offers this prayer as an expression of his deep concern, knowing that the sun will not wait for him, but at least confident that he may arrive before darkness falls.

The other prayer, 91, is offered by a priest or diviner, at a short ceremony before someone sets off on a journey. The request is a universal one for all travellers: to travel safely, be protected from death, misfortunes, enemies, thorns and lions, and have success. The officiant washes the traveller's body with a medicinal herb to give mystical protection in keeping with the requests of this prayer. The man can now go with confidence that 'Death does not come to him for whom prayer is made; death only comes to him who trusts in his own strength!' This prayer is a consolation and a blessing not only to the traveller himself, but to his family and friends as well. Through the ritual and accompanying prayer, they can also go with him in spirit, relying not on his or their own strength, but the strength of God (or the spiritual realm).

In all human activities, there is an element of the unforeseen, of chance, which lies beyond human powers or control. It is the co-operation of this dimension which man needs in his work, so that both the physical and the spiritual dimensions can harmonize to make man's work productive and a source of joy. Through these prayers, man's work is ritualized and sanctified. Therefore he dedicates seeds before sowing, invoking a hidden element so that he may reap a rich harvest; he returns thanks to God and the spiritual realm, normally at first fruits, for the good crop he is reaping; he prays for harmony with the earth, the forests and rivers on which he depends for his crops; he seeks permission to get fish from the river in peace and safety, for which reason he makes an offering or sacrifice to the river, in order that he may be in harmony with it and its teeming life; he seeks to put his trust in the spiritual realm as he goes on a journey, believing that it will be safe and successful. So man sanctifies his work, dedicates his activities, and acknowledges the strength and help of sources outside of his domain, sources that in African experience are spiritual. In this way, whether working in the fields, fishing in the river, or administering medicine to the sick, man is treading on a path in which the physical and the spiritual intermingle. The prayers that he offers are the threads which interweave the two realms and man is, *ipso facto*, the priest of the universe around him, rubbing the physical against the spiritual and the spiritual against the physical.

SOWING AND HARVESTING

66 Dedicating the seeds before sowing[1]

O Nyambe [God], you are the creator of all. Today we your creatures prostrate ourselves before you in supplication. We have no strength. You who have created us have all power. We bring you our seed and all our implements, that you may bless them and bless us also so that we may make good use of them by the power which comes from you, our creator.

67 Greeting God at sowing time[2]

Oh God! Receive the morning greetings!
Ancestors! Receive the morning greetings!
We are here on the chosen day,
We are going to sow the seed,
We are going out to cultivate.
Oh God! Cause the millet to germinate,
Make the eight seeds sprout,
And the ninth calabash.

Give a wife to him who has none!
And to him who has a wife without children
Give a child!
Protect the men against thorns,
Against snake-bites,
Against ill winds!

Pour out the rain,
As we pour water from a pot!
Millet! Come!

68 To the earth, forest and rivers at the sowing season[3]

O Earth, wherever it be my people dig, be kindly to them. Be fertile when they give the little seeds to your keeping. Let your generous warmth nourish them and your abundant moisture germinate them. Let them swell and sprout, drawing life from you, and burgeon under your fostering care: and soon we shall redden your bosom with the blood of goats slain in your honour, and offer to you the first fruits of your munificence, first fruits of millet and oil of sesame, of gourds and cucumbers and deep-mashed melons.

O trees of forest and glade, fall easily under the axe. Be gentle to my people. Let no harm come to them. Break no limb in your anger. Crush no one in your displeasure. Be obedient to the woodman's wishes and fall as he would have you fall, not perversely nor stubbornly, but as his axe directs. Submit yourselves freely to my people, as this tree has submitted itself to me. The axe rings, it bites into the tough wood. The tree totters and falls. The lightning flashes, its fire tears at the heart of the wood. The tree totters and falls. Before the lightning the tree falls headlong, precipitate, knowing neither direction nor guidance. But the woodman guides the tree where he wills and lays it to rest gently and with delibera-tion. Fall, O trees of forest and glade, even as this tree was fallen, hurting no one, obedient, observant of my will.

O rivers and streams, where the woodman has laid bare the earth, where he has hewn away the little bushes and torn out encumbering grass, there let your waters overflow. Bring down the leafy mould from the forest and the fertilizing silt from the mountains. When the rains swell your banks, spread out your waters and lay your rich treasures on our gardens.

Conspire together, O earth and rivers: conspire together O earth and rivers and forests. Be gentle and give us plenty from your teeming plenty. For it is I, Lomingamoi of the clan Idots, who speak, Keeper of the clan lands, Warden of the Forest, Master of the clan.

69 Sacrifice for a rich harvest[4]

Earth of my clan, accept this offering, I entreat you. Drink the blood which I pour on you. This goat, which is the goat of Lokuryamoi, is the price of your beauty. Deal kindly with Lokuryamoi, for he is our friend: and stranger though he be, grant him a harvest as rich as our own. Let Nagitak, the grain blight, shrink from touching his garden, and let the beasts of the forest and the birds of the air know that Lokuryamoi is as one of us.

70 Praise to God at harvest time[5]

LEADER: Mwene-Nyanga [God], you who have brought us rain and have given us a good harvest, let people eat grain of this harvest calmly and peacefully.

PEOPLE: Peace, praise ye, Ngai [God], peace be with us.
LEADER: Do not bring us any surprise or depression.
PEOPLE: Peace, praise ye, Ngai, peace be with us.
LEADER: Guard us against illness of people and our herds and flocks, so that we may enjoy this season's harvest in tranquillity.
PEOPLE: Peace, praise ye, Ngai, peace be with us.

71 Harvest thanksgiving[6]

This is yours, Kazooba [the Sun],
This is yours, Ruhanga [the Creator],
This is yours, Rugaba [the Giver].

72 For a bountiful harvest[7]

May our grain bear so much fruit that it be forgotten on the ground and that it lets fall along the path so much that next year when we go forth to seed, the fields and the pathways will be covered with green grain.

73 Litany for health at harvest time[8]

God! give us health,
And that it may be given to us strength
And that it may be given to us milk
If any man eats [it], may he like [it].
If the pregnant woman eats [it], may she like [it].

74 Invocation at a harvest festival[9]

God! give us health
God! give us raided cattle
God! give us the offspring
Of men and cattle.

75 For inviting a family spirit to the harvest[10]

See my lords
I have presented to you
I have given you this food.
Eat and be satisfied so that I may have health.

WORK OF A PRIEST,
MEDICINE-MAN AND DIVINER

76 Prayer of a priest-cum-diviner[11]

Ye divinities, come and accept this wine and drink.
Ye ghosts, come and accept this wine and drink.
Trees and *lianae*, come and accept this wine and drink.
God, who alone is great [*Nyankonpon Tweaduampon*, it was you
    who begat me, come and accept this wine and drink.
Spirit of the earth, come and accept this wine and drink.
Spirit of pools, come and accept this wine and drink.
Come, all of you, and accept this wine and drink.
Stand behind me with a good standing, and let me be possessed
    with a good possession.
Do not take water and retain it in your mouth when you speak to
    me [but address me clearly].
If any is sick, let me be able to tend him.
When I become possessed and divine [prophesy] for a chief,
Grant that what I have to tell him may not be bad.
Do not let me become impotent.
Do not let my eyes become covered over.
Do not let my ears become closed up.
Do not let my penis make a slave of my neck.

77 Invocation of a medicine-man[12]

O thou who rulest strength, thou Spirit of virile energy,
Thou canst do all, and without thee, I am powerless, I am powerless;
I who am consecrated to thee, I who am pledged to thee, O Spirit,
    from thee I get my strength, my power. Thou brought me the
    gift.
Spirit of force, I call thee. Acknowledge my call.
Come, come.
Thou must come, I gave thee what thou asked me,
The sacrifice has been given, sacrifice has been given in the forest;
Spirit, I am thine, thou art mine, come to me!

78 'God my Father, help us heal . . .'[13]

Jouk [God] my Father, help us heal this—
Since I have never taken anything from others,
I stole nothing in order to marry his mother—

I have no sin upon my soul.
Now I redeem the child from you with a ram.
Leave us the child, grant that he recover.

79 For effective medicine[14]

I have no saliva in my mouth. Thou art the possessor of saliva.
Come then and spit upon this medicine.

80 For medicinal herbs[15]

When pounding up the herbs, the MEDICINE-MAN *says:*

May he be well! Oh blessing! people of our family,
People of Nyeula, of Nxwakoli, of Qoma. May you look upon us,
  grandfather.

81 In administering medicine[16]

While rubbing in the medicine:

Today we are loosening you [i.e. freeing you from your sickness]
in the homestead of your family. Blessing. May you be well.

82 Invocation before an oracle[17]

Either:

Poison oracle, this man who has given me a test has many wives;
poison oracle, if he has not slept with these wives of his for many
months, kill the fowl; if he has slept with them, spare the fowl.

Or:

83

Poison oracle, this knife which you see, if I go to so-and-so's home
and make blood-brotherhood with him and he will show me his
medicine of the poison oracle, kill the fowl.

MINING, HUNTING, FISHING, AND TRAVELLING

84 In search of iron ore[18]

Asis [God], give us health.
Asis, give us iron wealth!

85 Divination invocation before a hunt[19]

Poison oracle, if I make my hunting squares in such and such a part
of the bush this year will I have a successful season? If it will be

successful, kill the fowl; if it will be spoilt by witchcraft spare the fowl.

86 A hunter's litany[20]

LEADER:	OTHER HUNTERS:
Akongo [God]:	Mokanga! (*word of agreement*)
Akongo of the ancestors:	Mokanga!
Akongo of the fathers:	Mokanga!
Our Akongo:	Mokanga!
We have come to your place,	
Give us animals:	Mokanga!
Many animals:	Mokanga!
Lest we go back with shame:	Mokanga!
To the women who have stayed behind:	Mokanga!
And lest the dead be disappointed:	Mokanga!
Let us track them, oh . . . . ee:	Mokanga!
Akongo:	Mokanga!
Akongo of the ancestors:	Mokanga!
Akongo of the fathers:	Mokanga!
Our Akongo:	Mokanga!
We rejoice:	Mokanga!
We thought you had made a mistake,	
Away where the women are in the village:	Mokanga!
They are also glad:	Mokanga!
Our ancestors have agreed:	Mokanga!
Our fathers have agreed:	Mokanga!
Akongo of our fathers has agreed:	Mokanga!

87 Hunters' request and thanksgiving[21]

O Mutalabala, Eternal One . . . we pray thee,
Let us kill today before sunset.

The others, falling on the ground, respond:
O Chief, today let us kill!

After succeeding in killing some animal, they cut up pieces of meat and the oldest man offers them to God, saying:
I thank thee for the meat which thou givest me.
Today thou hast stood by me.

88 A fisherman's prayer[22]

O Spirit, grant us a calm lake, little wind, little rain, so that the canoes may proceed well, so that they may proceed speedily.

89 'O river, I beg leave to take fish'[23]

O river, I beg leave to take fish from thee, as my ancestors did before me.
The antelope leaps and its young learns not to climb.
In such a manner the sons of men do as their fathers did.
O river, rise up, engulf your sharp-toothed monsters, and permit our young men to enter the water and enjoy themselves with the fish without being harmed.
If there is acceptance from you, then show it by accepting this baby chick. If not, if you cannot control the monsters, if one of them should harm our sons, then show it by refusing to accept this baby chick.

90 Traveller's request for delaying sunset[24]

You stone, may the sun not be quick to fall today. You stone, retard the sun on high so that I can arrive first at that homestead to which I journey, then the sun may set.

91 For a safe journey[25]

Gently! Smoothly! I say so. Death does not come to him for whom prayer is made; death only comes to him who trusts in his own strength! Let misfortune depart, let it go to Shiburi, and Nkhabelane. Let him travel safely; let him trample on his enemies; let thorns sleep, let lions sleep; let him drink water wherever he goes, and let that water make him happy, by the strength of this herb.

6 *War and adversity*

The contents of prayers connected with war are uniform: they ask for victory, safe return from war, and help in the difficulties caused by war. Throughout the world, man assumes that when he is at war, God is on his side and will grant him victory. Many prayers in this section reveal this attitude.

In prayer 92, the people are suddenly faced with an outbreak of war. They feel insecure: 'In our homeland . . . there is no forest where we may hide.' For that reason they turn to God who provides them with refuge: 'You are the forest wherein we may be safe.' But they do not sit down and wait for him to hide them from the enemy: they want their warriors to go and fight. Similarly, in the short invocation of 93, the people are terrified, and cry to God to 'fortify our arms', in order to meet the enemy.

Prayers 94 to 98 are made in preparation for war. People need courage as they depart for battle. For this reason they ask God to 'take me by the hand and lead me in safety' (94). This depicts them as being at the mercy of God who is their friend, father, and helper. In prayer 95 the warrior speaks as though he were addressing the enemy who once slew his relatives. He tells him that he has to 'avenge our own blood'. His spear must be on his side, and particularly so since he got it from his slain grandfather.

The prayer accompanying the war ritual round the sacred rock is very vivid (96). The people describe the expected rout of their enemy: 'We are poured on the enemy like a mighty torrent.' They are confident about winning the battle, hoping that their enemy will be bewildered: 'They look this way and that seeking escape, but our spears fall thickly upon them. Our spears cling to their bodies and they are routed.' But this anticipated victory is only possible if God is with them. Therefore they must pray: 'God of our fathers, guide our spears . . . Help us . . . Slay with us.' They sacrifice to him, striking the sacrificial animals with the same spears with which they will slay their enemy. They beseech God to 'let the enemy villages be desolate, (and) echo with the cry of mourning'.

The ritual prayer before battle (97) is difficult to interpret. One does not know the exact meaning of the 'white cow of heaven'. It is perhaps a sacrificial cow dedicated to victory. Perhaps it was originally captured in a cattle raid while it was only a calf. The time would now be ready for another, equally victorious raid which would bring additional cattle into the cattle-sheds. The prayer is one of anticipation of good fortune to add to the cows already captured. Though it is addressed to the 'white cow of heaven', it is invoked in the presence and hearing of God who would, in this and many other prayers, be the executor of the wishes expressed in the prayer. The next litany, number 98, demonstrates the same kind of sentiments but is expressly addressed to God before people go on a cattle raid. They ask, through the leader of their invocation, that God will grant them 'many cattle', 'much booty', and 'victory', and in faithful anticipation declare that 'He will grant' their requests. They are very confident of their victory.

Invocations 101 to 104 are made on behalf of soldiers already engaged in fighting. They are to raise hope for the safe return of fighting relatives. Those who remain at home must pray: 'Girls, be not silent . . . Tear out, tear out!' (101). The mothers and other relatives pray for the protection of young warriors that they might be spared to marry, establish families and 'beget children, very many' (102). To beget 'fathers and mothers' is an expression meaning sons and daughters who, in many African kinship systems, are like one's father and mother. The wife's prayer (104) for the safety of her husband expresses the common concern and feelings of wives throughout the world.

Prayers 105–110 are for deliverance. In prayer 105 the religio-political leader who led the Meru out of bondage asks for God's help in achieving such a difficult national task. Prayer 106 arose out of a situation of foreign domination: in this case the British who, together with the Egyptians, ruled the Sudan from 1899 to 1955. This is the only traditional prayer available in this collection, directed against the colonial occupation in any part of Africa.

Witchcraft is a dreaded evil in African societies, and in two prayers, 108 and 109, deliverance from it is sought. It is commonly held that most of people's sicknessess and misfortunes are caused by magic, witchcraft and sorcery.

It is rather surprising, therefore, that there are so few prayers that make reference to the supposed magical causes of evil. One explanation of this may be that, by detecting them through divination or suspicion as in prayer 109, people themselves deal directly with the witches and sorcerers. Witches would then be subjected to cleansing ordeals, severe beatings, or even death meted out by the community concerned. These steps give no time for prayers for protection against witches to be made.

Prayer 110 from Madagascar raises a problem rare to the African continent. It is addressed to God as the manifestation of evil, and asserts that 'one need not pray to a God who is good'. Evidently the people hold that the world was created by Zanar the good God, and Niang the wicked God. As the people's concern is with evil, they argue that 'one need not pray to a God who is good' (Zanar), but to the one who is causing havoc (Niang). They side with Zanar and plead: 'O Niang, don't destroy the good works of Zanar. . . . Do not torment the good among us.' Because Niang is supposed to be responsible for a whole range of evil and suffering, the people want to be delivered from him and they address their prayer to him accordingly. This form of dualism is generally absent among African peoples where evil is attributed to beings considerably inferior to God. Where God is associated with adversities of people, they are normally taken to be a form of punishment; but God himself is not thought to be wicked as such.

Other forms of adversity include hunger, famine, and general distress. In 111 and 112 the hungry man prays for food, he is so hungry that he can think of nothing else but food. The agonies of hunger are effectively described in 112: 'I lie down hungry, although others have eaten and lie down full.' Under such circumstances, the man would be content with a springbok, a polecat or a rock-rabbit. So he prays, 'Give me and I shall be grateful!'

Famine is always a major threat to human lives from time to time in many African societies. It is estimated that well over a quarter of a million people perished from the famines which swept across Sahel (the West African countries in the areas of, or bordering on, the Sahara) and Ethiopia, from 1972 to 1974, in spite of the modern methods of transporting food. Prayer 114 expresses the threats that many Africans have experienced: 'The famine is upon us ... The women and children are hungry.' With famine come also malnutrition, disease, epidemics and death. Therefore man must pray: 'Keep us free from sickness, epidemics and all evils.'

Prayers 115 and 116 do not specify the distress that calls for them. People want to laugh, to occupy their homes in peace, and to worship (115). Therefore they seek a restoration to those conditions of living. Prayer 116 is personalized, expressing a concern that Deng [God] should not abandon one to the powers of sickness. To be without spiritual assistance means to fall into distress and sickness. Therefore the plea is for God's continuing support.

Distress leads people to feel that 'God has forsaken us' (117). Probably these sentiments are caused by the impending death of an individual, or mass deaths through epidemic or famine.

Prayers 118, 119 and 120 express pain and anguish. In 118, the person cries pitifully to God: '. . . if only you would help me just this once! . . . I prostrate myself before you.' He is in agony. All he wants is to establish a home and to have children: 'I cry to you: Give me offspring.' Without a family of his own, he has nowhere to go: 'What shall I do, where shall I go?' This prayer articulates the feelings of many African people who hold that life is meaningless unless one bears children and establishes a home. Children are not only an insurance against old age, they also immortalize one after death. It is in the light of this concern that we must appreciate the feelings expressed in this prayer.

Prayer 119 gives vent to the deep sorrows caused by bereavement. The surviving people feel as if God has 'eaten' them (as if he has destroyed them in the death of their relative). Bereavement is so painful that, in prayer 120, the person concerned gets very angry with God and threatens, 'If I could meet with him, I would kill him.' Evidently this unbearable sorrow is caused by the death of an only child. The parent feels like 'dying in anguish', and in desperation tells God that he would run him through with a knife! This is a vivid, hyperbolic expression of one's distress and anguish. These three prayers explore the great spiritual depths of sorrow and anguish.

Misfortunes are a mystery, for which someone must be held responsible. In prayer 121 the person who is making a sacrifice is not sure whom to blame. He sways between the opinion of other people who say that the misfortunes in question have come from the living dead or bad spirits, and his own views that perhaps God has brought them about in punishment for wrong-doing. In any case he sacrifices to God and asks him to 'cause whoever or whatever is troubling us to go away. We want peace.' In the case of prayer 122, blame is laid on the earth which here is personified and acknowledged as providing good things. At the same time, the person blames the earth for the death of his wife, children, friends, and parents. The point he is making here is that these deceased relatives are buried in the earth, and this constitutes taking them from him, robbing him of his companions. This contrasts strongly with the opening of the prayer in which the man thanks or acknowledges the earth as being the source of his sustenance.

Prayer 123 has a personal touch as it expresses the law of 'an eye for an eye'. The kite is a bird of prey which is known for its sudden swooping and snatching away chicks, birds and small livestock, from people's hands or the ground. Here the person offering the prayer feels that his enemies might try to snatch something from him and he asks that, instead, they should suffer. The man is very defensive.

In these prayers about war and adversity, we see man at one of his weakest points of existence. His own powers have reached the nadir, and his only hope of survival is God or, in some few cases, other spiritual help.

WAR

92 At the outbreak of war[1]

We were at home and suddenly we heard the report that there was war. You are our Chief. That is why we have come to you to pray that you march at our head, in the war, to guide us. In our homeland, at Anlo, there is no forest where we may hide. But you, O Nyigibla of our ancestors, you are the forest wherein we may be safe. Call together, therefore, all your warriors, so that they may wage this war for us, for we have no strength whatever.

93 'Our enemies approach'[2]

Our enemies approach. O God, fortify our arms, grant us strength.

94 When departing for war[3]

Ruwa [God] my chief, take me by the hand and lead me in safety. Grant me also an ox, O chief, so that I may offer you sacrifice.

95 I go now into the fight[4]

O spear of my old grandfather,
I go now into the fight.
May my youths not stumble.
May the arrows fly into empty air,
   not touching the youths.

We are not entering into war without cause.
Once you slew my brother,
You slew my cousin.
You slew my grandfather, too.
May my spear today strike you in the back.
We've got to avenge our own blood.

96 At a war ritual round the sacred rock[5]

We are poured on the enemy like a mighty torrent;
We are poured like a river in spate when the rain is in the mountains.
The water hisses down the sands, swirling, exultant, and the tree that stood in its path is torn up quivering.
It is tossed from eddy to eddy.
We are poured on the enemy and they are bewildered.
They look this way and that seeking escape, but our spears fall thickly about them.
Our spears cling to their bodies and they are routed.
They look this way and that for deliverance, but they cannot escape us, the avengers, the great killers.

God of our fathers, guide our spears, our spears which thy lilac has touched.
They are anointed with sacrifice, with the sacrifice of unblemished kids, consecrated and hallowed by the Nightjar of good omen.
Help us, high spirit. Slay with us.
Let death come to their ranks, let the villages mourn their lost warriors.
Let their villages be desolate, let them echo with the cry of mourning.
We shall return rejoicing; and the lowing of cattle is in our ears.
The lowering of innumerable cattle will make glad our hearts.

97 Ritual prayer before battle[6]

White cow of heaven,
You have fed in rich pastures
And you who were small have grown great.
White cow of heaven,
Your horns have curved full circle and are joined as one.
White cow of heaven,
We throw at your feet the dust
Which your feet have overseen
That the udders of our cows may be heavy
And that our women may rejoice.

98 Before a cattle raid[7]

LEADER (*recites*):   OTHER PEOPLE (*respond*).

Let us say to Engai [God]:
Grant us many cattle!   He will grant it.

Grant us life!	He will grant it.
Grant us health and happiness!	He will grant it.
Grant us victory!	He will grant it.
Grant us much booty!	He will grant it.

99 After being defeated in a raid[8]

God! have we said: 'Oiyo'.
Have we prayed thee, 'Emuro'.

100 Invocation after a cattle raid[9]

God! cover for us these here.
Have we prayed thee,
Guard for us these here.

101 Litany for warriors at war[10]

LEADER:	God! God! tear out
GROUP CHORUS:	The brand-marks of the people!
LEADER:	Tear out, tear out
GROUP CHORUS:	The brand-marks of the people!
LEADER:	Girls, be not silent.
GROUP CHORUS:	It is being prayed to God.
LEADER:	Tear out, tear out
GROUP CHORUS:	The brand-marks of the people!

102 For young warriors[11]

Ehe, ehe, may they be loved, ehe, by all,
May they beget fathers and mothers,
May they have goats and cattle,
May they beget children, very many.

103 For safe return from war[12]

LEADER:	The God to whom I pray, and he hears.
GROUP CHORUS:	The God to whom I pray for offspring.
LEADER:	I pray the heavenly bodies which have risen.
GROUP CHORUS:	The God to whom I pray for offspring.
LEADER:	Return hither our children (from war),
GROUP CHORUS:	Return hither our children.

104 For a husband in war[13]

Let him be saved with those who went with him

Let him stand firm with them
Let him return from the battle with them
Whether they capture them,
Whether they bring them home,
Whether they stab each other,
Come and see them.

DELIVERANCE

105 National deliverance[14]

One body and possessor of strength,
Give me thy help,
That I may lead this people of thine
Free from all their sufferings.

106 Deliverance from foreign domination[15]

Stars and moon which are in the heavens,
Blood of deng which you have taken [of the Dinka],
You have not summoned the ants [*Nuer*] of deng capriciously [in vain],
Blood of deng which you have taken,
The wing of battle on the river bank is encircled by [ostrich] plumes.
Dayim, son of God, strike the British to the ground,
Break the steamer on the Nile and let the British drown,
Kill the people on the mountains,
Kill them twice [i.e. two years in succession],
Do not slay them jestingly.
Mani goes with a rush,
He goes on for ever,
The sons of Jagei [Nuer people] are proud in the byres,
Proud that they always raid the Dinka.

107 Deliverance by departed mother[16]

O mother, we beseech thee to deliver us,
Look after us, look after [our] children;
Thou who art established at Ado.

108 'If it be a witch. . . .'[17]

Repeat my words ee! You flesh of my father, I call you in my prayer because of the man who came to bewitch and left his fishing-spear behind. Therefore, I call you to hear me. A man became sick because of a witch. And I have thought thus: it if be a child who brought the spear and forgot it, then I have no quarrel with him. But if it be a witch who came to bewitch, then you flesh of my father show him your strength, that he may see for himself what you can do. I have no long speech to make to you, I shall soon be silent.

109 Divination prayer for detecting witches[18]

You, Tembong of the clan Latum, the place where God was born.
When he returned to the village, he carried lumps of Kaolin.
If truly the suspect is a witch, kill her!
If she is innocent, save her!

110 In wrestling with good and evil[19]

O Zanar [God, Creator], not to thee do we lift our voices.
One need not pray to a God who is good.
But we must placate the wrath of Niang [Creator].
O Niang! wicked and powerful God, let not the thunder rumble over our poor heads; let not the furious sea break over its banks; spare our tender fruits; do not burn the rice before it has flowered; don't bring catastrophe and suffering down on our women; force no woman to see the hope of her old age borne away and buried at sea.
O Niang! Don't destroy the good works of Zanar.
Thou rulest over the wicked and their number is sufficiently great.
Do not torment the good among us.

ADVERSITY

111 A hunter's prayer for food[20]

Ho! Moon, lying there,
Let me kill a springbok,
Tomorrow
Let me eat a springbok;
With this arrow,
Let me shoot a springbok!

112 Prayer of a hungry man[21]

God of our fathers, I lie down without food,
I lie down hungry,
Although others have eaten and lie down full.

Even if it be but a polecat, or a little rock-rabbit,
Give me and I shall be grateful!
I cry to God, Father of my ancestors.

113 In time of starvation[22]

Mbamba [God], Kiara, you have denied us rain, grant us rain so that
we may not die. Deliver us from death by starvation. For thou art
our Father and we are thy children. Thou hast created us. Why,
then, dost thou wish us to die? Give us maize, bananas, and beans.
Thou hast given us feet to walk with, arms to work with, and even
sons: grant us also rain so that we may harvest!

114 'The famine is upon us'[23]

Sie, Dyohourete, Dyorfoute, Dyolinnte, and all the priests of the
   Earth who lived before me have observed this custom, and now
   it is my turn.
The famine is upon us. We have no millet, maize, or beans.
Our cattle, sheep, and goats are dead, as are our chickens.
The women and children are hungry.
Therefore we have decided to set up our homes in this unoccupied
   place.
O nurturing Earth, we offer thee this chicken; accept it, we beseech
   thee, and in exchange give us bountiful harvest, numerous herds
   and flocks, and many children.
Keep us free from sickness, epidemics and all evils.

115 Litany in time of distress[24]

Who will laugh?
The cattle-ant and the ant of the boat.
Who will possess a homestead?
Unite the ants to a head.
Who will laugh?
The cattle-ant and the ant of the boat.
The ants have gone to Deng [as their] head
And the fish-lord has not appeared.
Let us worship.
Our Dura-Lord has not appeared.
Let us worship.

116 'Do not forsake me'[25]

Deng my father, Deng of surpassing greatness,

My father Deng, a great person through the ages.
Great Deng refuses [to listen], Great Deng refuses [to help];
If not honoured, he is offended, indifferent.
My father Deng, do not forsake me,
My father Deng, do not abandon me to the Powers [of sickness].

117 'God has forsaken us'[26]

God has forsaken us,
The Creator of the sun refuses us life.
O cold white moon,
The Creator of the sun refuses us life.

118 Kwambaza: a cry for help[27]

O Imana [God] of Urundi [Ruanda], if only you would help me!
O Imana of pity, Imana of my father's home [country], if only you
   would help me!
O Imana of the country of the Hutu and the Tutsi, if only you would
   help me just this once!
O Imana, if only you would give me a homestead [*rugo*] and children!
I prostrate myself before you, Imana of Urundi [Ruanda].
I cry to you: Give me offspring, give me as you give to others!
Imana, what shall I do, where shall I go?
I am in distress: where is there room for me?
O Merciful, O Imana of mercy, help this once!

119 Chura Intimba: 'To forge heart-heaviness'[28]

As for me, Imana [God] has eaten me, yo–ho–o!
As for me, he has not dealt with me as with others.
With singing I would sing, yo–ho–o!
If only my brother [or whoever died] was with me.
Sorrow is not to hang the head mourning,
Sorrow is not to go weeping.
As for me, Imana has eaten me, yo–ho–o!
As for me, he has not dealt with me as with others;
If he had dealt with me as with others
I could be as Rwirahirabamurinda [Scorner-of-enemies].
Woe is me! Yo–ho–o!

120 Intimba: heart-heaviness[29]

I don't know for what Imana [God] is punishing me: if I could meet
with him I would kill him. Imana, why are you punishing me? Why

have you not made me like other people? Couldn't you even give me one little child, Yo-o-o! I am dying in anguish! If only I could meet you and pay you out! Come on, let me kill you! Let me run through with a knife! O Imana, you have deserted me! Yo-o-o! [Woe is me!]

121 For removal of misfortune[30]

God, this sacrifice is to you. Others say that ancestors or some other bad spirits have brought misfortune upon us. But I believe that it is you. If you have brought this trouble upon us, take it away. If I'm wrong, cause whoever or whatever is troubling us to go away. We want peace.

122 'Have mercy, O Earth'[31]

Have mercy upon me, O Earth! It is upon thee that I dwell, it is thou that givest to me my food and the water that I drink, it is thou that givest me clothes. Be merciful towards me, O Earth! Thou takest from me the wife without whom I cannot live, thou takest from me the children that are my joy, takest my friends that are dear to me, and takest even my father and mother.

123 'If I am hated, then I hate'[32]

If I am hated, then I hate,
If I am loved, then I love,
If a kite swoops upon what is mine
Then it regrets it, seeing what I am
It trembles inwardly.
If a kite swoops upon what is mine, ee
Its wing breaks.
When it sees, it fears and trembles.

7 Life's journey

In considering prayer 118 in the previous chapter, we saw the importance that African peoples attach to procreation and offspring. As life's journey starts with procreation, there are several prayers connected with fertility and childbirth. The first of these, 124, is a litany on behalf of a woman who has no children. The friends, relatives and neighbours assemble to pray with a unanimous voice that God will 'grant children to her'. The repetition of this phrase emphasizes the concern shared by everyone over the childless woman.

There is a general feeling in African societies that to get a son is extremely important. It is the son who, in patrilineal societies, carries on the biological line of his forefathers. The son should be present at and normally presides over family rituals. It is the son who sets up a new home. Therefore, the desire to beget a son is great for social, economic and religious reasons. This concern comes out plainly in prayer 125 where a mother or father asks to be granted a son, promising in return to show gratitude to God by offering a goat.

The birth of a child can be, at times, a difficult event for the mother. In prayer 126 the people ask their forefathers 'who are of the near and far past' to grant a safe delivery of a baby. The occasion seems to be very tense and the husband even offers to be punished if that would help the situation. The wife's own father adds a special plea. The midwife, too, has her own prayer (127), which she offers in connection with her work. It is addressed to the infant, but the understanding is that God will keep the baby free from sickness and cause it to grow into an adult: 'Settle down, and may you have work.' This repeated formula is a kind of blessing, covering the entire life from birth through adulthood. In some African societies, pregnancy and childbirth are connected with the spirits, especially the living dead, who may be held responsible for the actual pregnancy or may be partially reincarnated in the infant. For this reason the midwife makes reference to 'the world of the spirits', because it is as if the child is coming out of the spirit world to that of human beings.

The birth of twins has generally caused special attention in many

African societies. It is alleged that in some cases either or both of the twins were formerly killed, because their birth was regarded as a bad omen. In other cases twins enjoy extra attention and special religious rites are performed to welcome them. Prayer 128 is made at one such ceremony where a bull is sacrificed to God and he is asked to 'let them live'. Prayer 129 is a prayer of purification at the ceremony marking the birth of twins. At this ceremony God is asked to keep both the twins and their mother well, and to prosper the people among whom the twins have been born. It is an occasion of joy, for the birth of the twins is as if 'God has come upon us. We accept thee. Stay, stay thou with us.'

Naming ceremonies are held in many African societies. We have here, however, only one prayer (131) offered at the naming ceremony. It asks that the child should 'grow up', and look after his ageing grandparents and parents.

Initiation ceremonies are performed in a number of African communities, involving circumcision and clitoridectomy, admission into adulthood, admission into 'secret' societies, or other major changes in one's life. In prayer 132 we have an example of a prayer which accompanies such an occasion. It is set in a very joyful mood, and involves a recitation by the leader and a group response. In this litany the younger and older age group show how confident they are that God will grant them their requests. The reciter calls out: 'Evil is going away', to which the group response is: 'It has gone!' Then he continues: 'Well-being is with us', and the reply is 'It is!' Both sides repeatedly shout with confidence that well-being will continue to be with them. The litany ends with words of confidence: 'God has heard' the prayer to which the sky has been witness. The sky is the dwelling place of God and, since it is always present, symbolizes his enduring presence. It is reported that when this prayer is being offered, one leader may succeed another until there is a general feeling that enough praying has been offered. Then the sacrificial animals are divided up, cooked by the initiates, and eaten by members of the older age group who may offer some to the initiate. This done, the people disperse until the second initiation ceremonies take place at the homestead of each initiate.

Prayer 133 is offered at another type of initiation ceremony. It states that the young initiates have come for their initiation, and asks that God may 'penetrate them with thy shadow'. This is a symbolic way of asking him to protect them and keep them alive. God is their Father, and the initiates are his children. The other initiation prayer, 134, says nothing about the candidates, but it accompanies an offering made on their behalf.

Two prayers, 135 and 136, are invocations at a simple ceremony to mark the onset of menstruation. An offering of wine is made to God and the departed, and then a request is made. Since menstruation heralds procreation, the young girl should be preserved to bear children. It is useless if she were to come to the threshold of procreation only to die before fully entering: 'Do not have permitted her to menstruate only to die.'

Only one prayer, 137, on the occasion of an engagement to marriage is available. It is addressed to the forefathers of the chief and invites them to assemble for the banquet. It is believed that the living dead are interested and involved in such major family matters as initiation, engagement and marriage ceremonies. In this prayer it is clear that the people are very much aware of the presence of the departed. The chief addresses them face to face as he invites them to 'sit and eat, you and your people'. I have no prayers offered specifically at the wedding ceremonies as such.

Death generates a lot of feelings, and people seem to express those feelings through prayers, among other ways. Twelve prayers (138–149) are gathered together in connection with death, though many more are scattered throughout the collection. In these prayers we see the pain, the sorrow, the agonies, the despair, the bewilderment and the anguish experienced by people at a time of bereavement. While entering into the grief of those who weep in these prayers one is aware of their certainty that life continues beyond the grave.

Prayer 138 agonizes over the death of an infant, committing the spirit of the child to the 'mother who dwells in the land of spirits'. The 'mother' is thanked for letting the child be borne, and is requested to give people another child to replace the dead one. The prayer is accompanied by food offers to the spirit of the dead child, in the hope that it will settle in the spirit world and not cause trouble to the living.

The dying man who prays in 140 is brave and generous. He wants to return love for any hatred he may have suffered. He calls upon God as his Creator and Father to help him. He dies a spiritually pure death, without malice and with only love in his heart.

The funeral recitation (141) is a great psalm reflecting on the brevity of life. This brevity is summarized in the very first two lines: 'The creature is born, it fades away, it dies, And comes then the great cold.' To every form of life whether it be of man, bird, or fish, there 'comes then the great cold', the closing of life in death. Yet for man, there is hope of continuity of life beyond death, for death frees 'the prisoner', and the shadow or spirit goes on living. God superintends the life of man, and for that reason people cry unto him to sustain them in the shortness of life.

In the deep sorrow of bereavement, people cry that God has 'called too soon' (142). This is a universal feeling about the death of loved ones. Yet, in keeping with African beliefs, the departed is still alive, therefore God is asked to give him water and fire; while the departed is requested to prepare a place for those who are still alive. It is the hope of the living that they will be reunited with the departed: 'In a little while we shall reach, Let us reach each other.'

Prayer 143 is a polite rebuke to God, for making people subject to death. The praying person acknowledges that the works of God are good, but sorrow has struck because of death. He tells God that he should 'have planned in some way that we would not be subject to death'. Again this is a universal wish of many at moments of bereavement. In prayer 144, the departed forefathers are blamed for taking away the dead man. The living are as dead because of grief, so they ask that they be left in peace, even if they have to weep over the departed. Death, however, makes the survivors resolve to 'help each other in our pain'.

We have already seen prayers (68 and 69) in which man wants to be in harmony with the earth, the forests and the rivers, before he utilizes them. In prayers 145–148 the same desire to establish a good relationship is expressed, particularly since the body of the dead person will remain in the earth for good. Man therefore prays to the earth: 'We have come to beg you for this spot, So that we may dig a hole.' Prayer 146 reminds us again of the belief in the continuity of life after death, and the abiding presence of the living dead. At the burial ceremony, 'The spirits of the dead are thronging together, Like swarming mosquitoes in the evening.' The departed are evidently thought to be interested in what the living are doing, and join in the major activities of their surviving families. The living dead according to this prayer 'wait for him who will come', and welcome him into their midst. The prayer ends with a difficult statement that 'God will be with his children'. This could mean that the dead are in a special sense God's children. We cannot interpret it to mean that the dead go to 'heaven' to be with God. It could also mean that at the time of bereavement, the surviving people need to feel the fatherly presence of God, with his parental care. At this moment of loss, they feel very much in need of God's presence just as the troubled child needs the presence of father or mother.

The series of invocations in number 147 reveals, among other things, people's relationships with the departed. They tell the newly dead that they love and respect him—these being two very important values in African societies. When the people ask the departed to 'give us rain', etc., this is not to be taken in the literal sense. What they mean is to ask the departed not to wish bad things for the living. Rain, good harvest, long life, large families: all these constitute well-being, and death should not disrupt that well-being. The people, presumably, pour libation on the grave as they continue to address the departed to 'give us long life, many children, some wives and well-being'. They have hope that the dead father 'will come back'. This means that children will be born as part-reincarnation of the dead father, which will be taken to mean that he had not altogether abandoned the living. The final line is not a prayer but an injunction or piece of advice to the young men at the burial ceremony, to make sure that wild animals or witches do not have access to the corpse. It is believed in many African societies that witches dig up corpses for use in their hideous activities, but one has the impression that this actually happens only very rarely.

A bereaved wife addresses her deceased husband at the time of his burial, in prayer 148. Other relatives join in using similar words. It is a moving prayer, showing the agonies of bereavement: 'Why have you done thus to me? Where shall I go?' And this is the universal question that many would pose. It is a painful rhetorical question for which no answer is ever forthcoming.

The mortuary hymn (149) repeats people's concern with life when death strikes. They hope that 'life is revived. . . . They cry aloud with joy.' But because death makes them feel humble and small, they speak of themselves as 'the ants', and consider themselves to be 'simple people (who) do not understand how their lives are supported.' And in the face of death, man may be considered as insignificant as an ant.

FERTILITY AND CHILDBIRTH

124 'Grant children to her' [Litany for fertility][1]

LEADER: Thou, Jouk [God], who art our Father and hast
           created all of us,

           Thou knowest this woman is ours, and we wish her to
           bear children—

ALTOGETHER: Grant children to her!

LEADER: Should we die tomorrow, no children of ours will remain—

ALTOGETHER: Grant children to her!

LEADER: If she bears a son, his name will be the name of his grandfather.

If she bears a daughter, her name will be the name of her grandmother.

ALTOGETHER: Grant children to her!

LEADER: Would it be displeasing to thee if many children surrounded us?

Spirit of the father, spirit of the grandfather, you who dwell now in the skies,

Are you displeased that we ask for children?

ALTOGETHER: Grant children to her!

LEADER: Should we die without them, who will guard the family?

Your name and ours shall be forgotten upon the earth.

ALTOGETHER: Grant us this night good dreams,

That we will die leaving many children behind us.

125 'Grant me a son'[2]

I pray to you, grant me a son.

If you grant my prayer, I will show you my gratitude and offer a goat up to you.

126 For a safe delivery[3]

ALL ASSEMBLED: O fathers and ancestors, and all who are of the near and far past, bear witness: we cry to thee [God] to let this child be safely born.

HUSBAND: If I have sinned, be merciful, and if thou canst not be merciful then punish me, slay me: but heal this woman and let this child live.

FATHER *of the woman*: This is my daughter: she is in your hands: spare her life, and give her a living child.

127 A midwife's prayer[4]

I take you out of the world of the spirits. Do not be sick, settle down, and may you have work.

Here is this cloth for you, and now a pillow and now a bed: receive these to take you out of the world of the spirits. Settle down, and may you have work.

128 Prayer for twins[5]

Thou, Nhialic [God], it is thou alone who created them,
Thou alone didst bring them: no man hates them.

Thou, Nhialic, look on life mercifully;
No man is mighty, thou art mighty.
Accept the bull, I have paid you the wage,
Let them live!

129 'God, stay with us favourably'[6]

Pu! Thou, God, hast come upon us. We accept thee. Stay, stay thou with us favourably. May the children be well; may their mother be well. Any animal that comes before us, let our spears fall on its body. Any man who seeks us, let us kill him and rejoice.

130 At the ceremony of washing an infant[7]

God! give us health.
God! protect us.
And you our spirits, protect for us this child.

To the child:
Become a man! throw away the cough.

NAMING AND INITIATION

131 At the naming ceremony[8]

Father and divinity Bosomtwe (or whichever), my child so-and-so has begotten a child and he has brought him to me, and I now call him after myself naming him so-and-so; grant that he grow up and continue to meet me here, and let him give me food.

132 Litany for the initiation ceremony[9]

(*The Gazelles* is the name of the newly initiated group: *The Mountains* is the name of the inducting group. Ngipian is the territorial section.)

LEADER:	GROUP RESPONSE:
The Gazelles. I say the Gazelles.	
There are Gazelles.	There are!

These people, the Gazelles which are here, they have become big (i.e. grown up).   They have become big!

The Mountains also. There are Mountains. There are!   There are! / There are!

The Karimojong also, they are.   They are!

There are Karimojong.   There are!

Cattle as well. The cattle of the Mountains. They are.   They are!

The cattle, the cattle of the Mountains, they become fat.   They are fat!

They become fat. Do they not become fat?   They are fat!

The land. This land here. Does it not become good?   It is good!

In this country there are Gazelles.   There are!

The Mountains also, they are.   They are!

Ngipian also. They are here, are they not?   They are!

In this land here, they are.   They are!

There is well-being in our country, is there not?   There is!

It is here.   It is!

Yes. Evil is going away.   It has gone!

It is leaving.   It has gone!

Well-being is with us.   It is!

It will always be with us, will it not?   It will!

It will.   It will!

Will it not?   It will!

God has heard.   He has heard!

He has heard.   He has heard!

The sky, the cloud-spotted sky here, it has heard!   It has heard!

133 To him who is deathless[10]

Thou who art deathless,
Who knowest not death,
Who livest always,
Never feeling the cold sleep,
Thy children have come
To gather around thee.

O Father, gird up thy strength,
Penetrate them (the young initiates) with thy shadow,

O Father of our race,
O Father who never dies.

134 Invocation at circumcision offering[11]

Wele [God], you bless this cock which I am holding. I'm giving it
to all those who have passed on for their use. Come, this is your
[plural] white cock. You may use it. I'm placing it here in the basket.

135 At the first menstruation ceremony[12]

Nyankonpon Tweaduapon Nyame [Supreme Sky God, who alone
   is great], upon whom men lean and do not fall, receive this wine
   and drink.
Earth Goddess, whose day of worship is a Thursday, receive this
   wine and drink.
Spirit of our ancestors, receive this wine and drink.
This girl child whom God has given to me, today the Bara state has
   come upon her.
O mother who dwells in the land of ghosts, do not come and take
   her away, and do not have permitted her to menstruate only to die.

136 For fertile puberty

Receive this loin cloth, and sponge, and eggs, and do not let this
infant have come to puberty [only] to die.

137 At the engagement of a chief's daughter[13]

O father, forebear of my daughter, this is the ox that we are sacrificing for you. Go up to the mountains, call your servants, assemble
all your people for this banquet, all your warriors. This is your ox,
chosen for you by your people. Sit and eat it, you and your people.

DEATH

138 At the death of an infant[14]

O Mother who dwells in the land of spirits, receive this *eto* and eggs
and eat. We thank you very much that you permitted this one to
come, but we beg you for a new one. And you infant who are gone,
receive your eggs and give to your old mother saying: 'Let one
come again but permit it to remain.'

The MOTHER *of the dead child says:*
Spirit, eat on the path, do not eat in my belly.

139 Commending a dying person[15]

Our God, who has brought us [to this world],
May she take you.

140 Prayer of a dying man[16]

And though I behold a man hate me,
I will love him.
O God, Father, help me, Father!
O God, Creator, help me, Father!
And even though I behold a man hate me,
I will love him.

141 Funeral recitation[17]

LEADER:

GROUP RESPONSE:

The creature is born, it fades away, it dies,
And comes then the great cold.

It is the great cold of the night, it is the dark.

The bird comes, it flies, it dies,
And comes then the great cold.

It is the great cold of the night, it is the dark.

The fish swims away, it goes, it dies,
And comes then the great cold.

It is the great cold of the night, it is the dark.

Man is born, he eats and sleeps. He fades away,
And comes then the great cold.

It is the great cold of the night, it is the dark.

And the sky lights up, the eyes are closed,
The star shines.

The cold down here, the light up there.

Man is gone, the prisoner is freed,
The shadow has disappeared.

The shadow has disappeared.

Khmvoum [God], Khmvoum, hear our call.

Khmvoum, Khmvoum, hear our call.

142 'God, you have called too soon'[18]

Would it were not today!
God, you have called too soon!
Give him water, he has left without food;
Light a fire, he must not perish.

Addressing the dead person:
Prepare a place for us,
In a little while we shall reach,
Let us reach each other.

143 Sorrow brought about by death[19]

O great Nzambi [God], what thou hast made is good, but thou hast
brought a great sorrow to us with death. Thou shouldest have
planned in some way that we would not be subject to death. O
Nzambi, we are afflicted with great sadness.

144 'Let us weep softly'[20]

You, my forefathers, you have congregated here today. Do you not
see this? You have taken him with you. I am alone now. I am dead,
I implore you, who are so far, since he has gone back to you, let us
remain in peace. He has not left us with hate. Let us weep softly
over him, in peace. Let us help each other in our pain, even his
wife's parents.

145 Prayer at grave-digging[21]

Earth, whose day is Thursday,
Receive this wine and drink,
It is your grandchild . . . that has died,
We have come to beg you for this spot
So that we may dig a hole.

146 Committing the dead body to the grave[22]

The gates of the underworld are closed.
Closed are the gates.

The spirits of the dead are thronging together
Like swarming mosquitoes in the evening,
like swarming mosquitoes.
Like swarms of mosquitoes dancing in the evening,
When the night has turned black, entirely black,
When the sun has sunk, has sunk below.

when the night has turned black
the mosquitoes are swarming
like whirling leaves, dead leaves in the wind.

Dead leaves in the wind,
they wait for him who will come
for him who will come and will say:
'Come' to the one and 'Go' to the other,
And God will be with his children.
And God will be with his children.

147 Burial invocations[23]

(a) Pray do not get angry, we love you, we respect you, be happy
while you stay in the Lahara.

(b) Give us rain when the hibernating time comes, give us a
plentiful crop, a spry old age, some children, some wives, give
us well-being.

(c) See this water, do not get angry, forgive us, give us rain when
the hibernating time comes and a plentiful crop. Should wind
come from the west or east, from the south or north, let it be
favourable.
Give us a long life, many children, some wives, and well-being.

(d) Our father is dead, we have been told, he is dead. But he will
come back. (Young men, close the grave and do not let a witch or a
hyena or a wild beast carry the corpse away.)

148 In desperation of bereavement[24]

My husband, you have abandoned me.
My master is gone and will never return.
I am lost.
I have no hope.
For you used to fetch water and collect firewood for me.
You used to clothe and feed me with good things.
Why have you done thus to me?
Where shall I go?

149 A mortuary hymn[25]

Mother of *deng* [a spirit of the air], the ants [the Nuer] ransom their
lives from thee,
Mother of *dengkur*, the ants ransom their lives from thee,
The mother of *dengkur* brings life,

The mother of *dengkur* brings me life,
Life is revived.
She brings life and our children play,
They cry aloud with joy,
With the life of the mother of *deng*, with the life of the mother of
    deng.
The pied crows are given life and are filled.
Our speech is good, we and *buk*,
Our speech is excellent;
The country of the people is good,
We journey on the path of the *pake*.
We are here, we and *buk deang*,
Buk, mother of *deng*, the ants ransom their lives from thee,
Mother of *dengkur*, the ants ransom their lives from thee.
We give thee red blood.
The ants of *deng* are simple people, they do not understand how
    their lives are supported.
Let all the people of the cattle camps bring tobacco to the river.

8 *The spirits*

In African religious beliefs and practices, the reality of the spirits is taken for granted. They may be considered variously, so that there are spirits associated with the earth and those associated with the air or sky. There are spirits which were created by God originally in spirit forms, while other spirits are the remaining portion of what were once human beings. Some spirits are regarded as higher in status than others, and are often referred to as divinities. The human spirits of people who died four or five generations ago are spoken of in recent literature as the living dead (a term originally coined by the author and given great currency by other writers).

In these 17 prayers we see people expressing their relationships to the spirits in various ways. Some of the prayers are made to accompany offerings and libations for the living dead. The prayers, offerings and libations are symbols of remembering the departed, and an indication of the welcome or hospitality extended to them by the living members of their families. We have already indicated in an earlier chapter that the traditional concept of the family, according to African peoples, is one that includes the living, those yet to be born and the large number of the departed. Some other prayers are forms of incantations for warding off any malicious spirits. There are prayers, too, which are made as part of exorcisms in order to chase out spirits who are supposed to cause sickness, and those who possess people. A few prayers are addressed to spirits associated with nature or animals, and are aimed at avoiding any careless use of nature's riches.

Prayers 150 to 156 are addressed to the living dead. In them we see people speaking as though they were face to face with the spirits of the departed. Prayer 150 is a good illustration of people's concern with remembering the living dead. Where offerings of food and drink are placed before them, the offering affords people the opportunity to tell the departed that their names have not been forgotten, and to seek favour from them: 'let the people have good health . . . lions and leopards, let them be killed', etc. People want to remain in harmony with their departed relatives, and to lead peaceful lives. To forget the living dead would upset the harmony of life, it would generate ill-health, failure in hunting, difficult childbirth, and other evils. Normalizing relations with the departed ensures continued peace and tranquillity in the daily affairs of human life.

Prayer 151 simply invites the spirits to come and take the food given to them by their living relatives. There are no special requests from people. Probably the spirits in question have been neglected for a while by their relatives, making other spirits laugh at them. Now negligence is being remedied, and the family spirits may scorn the others because a cow, here being offered to them, makes them truly better off than other spirits who probably were offered only smaller animals like sheep or goats.

The departed is being reminded, in prayer 152, that his dwelling place is no longer with human beings, 'it is with the beasts', and so people instruct the spirit of the dead to keep away from them. The only way to return in a welcome manner is through the birth of a baby which is regarded as a partial form of reincarnation.

The spirit is told: 'there are babes about to be born, choose for thyself one of them', and it is enjoined to make its return to human society that way. But it has to be careful lest it makes a bad choice, 'for the babe you choose will become a person of honour and of good report'. Having chosen one baby, it cannot abandon it afterwards. So now, it is categorically told: 'Thine is the power and thou wilt go as the spirits intended, but go in peace and remember mercy.'

Prayer 153 is set in the context of making a fellowship sacrifice for one's departed parents and other close spirits. The man slays some oxen, and tells the living dead: 'Let us eat them together, you, father and mother. . . . I possess them for you.' He takes the opportunity to indicate his wishes, namely that he wants the family to remain in good health. Prayer 154 also accompanies offerings and sacrifices to the living dead, and expresses people's wishes to be kept free from sickness and safe from all evil, and to enjoy prosperity. People believe that being in harmony with the departed brings well-being in other areas of their life.

The man who is offering prayer number 156 is getting impatient with the spirits. He tells them: 'Have patience: I wish to cut grain until I have earned a goat to offer up to you.' The spirits have been bothering him, asking for a goat, but he is not yet ready with one. He warns them that if they continue to pester him they will never receive anything from him, and the other spirits will jeer at them. In a note of *conditio sine qua non*, he throws the ball to their court: 'Therefore, watch over me and you will receive your due.' In this prayer man is on an equal footing with the spirits, and may even put them at his mercy. He may respect them, as his forefathers, but clearly he is not frightened of them and if they become a nuisance he will simply forget them, to their misery and shame.

That man is not really afraid of the spirits is illustrated clearly in the prayers for warding off spirits and exorcizing them more or less as he wishes. In prayer 157, the spirits are given a goat sacrifice and told to 'go and don't return'. In 158, the spirit which is supposed to be causing havoc is simply ordered: '. . . you must leave this person alone, and you must leave this village.' Then the medicine-man performing the rite leads it away, and that is the end of the game. A similar fate comes upon the spirit of the witch in prayer 159, as the medicine-man categorically tells it: 'Come up, come out, I command you.'

In prayer 161 we see an even more dramatic encounter between man and the spirits. The diviners (or medicine-men) give a kind of lecture to the spirit of someone who has died. They tell the spirit that it has allowed the man to die ('fall to the ground'). So now they have 'come today to drive you away from the soul whose destiny you ruled. You will no longer be respected. . . . You, too, will be killed today.' Evidently the background to this form of ceremony is the belief that each person has a guardian spirit, and this must be asked to leave once it has let its client die. I do not understand prayer 162, but the diviner is addressing either the guardian spirit, or the personification of death, asking it to depart from among the people—one death is enough. Prayer 163 is an exorcism formula. It is to be noted that in it, tribal spirits are called upon to help in driving out the unwanted spirits.

The maker of the talking drum must, according to prayers 164 and 165, inform the spirits of the tree and of the elephant that he intends to use these items for making the drum. The spirits must of necessity move to other trees and other elephants. But they have to be removed peacefully and not to be evoked suddenly. So, 'the divine drummer announces' that he is going to cut down the tree and cut off the elephant ear. The spirits are told that they 'will understand' this action, and move off quietly to find other dwelling places. In prayer 166, the earth is personified and addressed, so that man may remain in harmony with it since man depends so much on it both while he is alive and when he has died (since it receives his body.)

REMEMBERING THE DEPARTED

150 Remembering the living dead[1]

First at an offering to the living dead
ALL *sing:*

Your food is here, here it is,
Let the children have good health,
Their wives, let them have children
So that your names may not be obliterated.
Your chicken is here;
Today we give you blood, here it is.
Let us have good health.

Then this litany ends the ceremony of presenting food to the departed:

LEADER: Let there be silence, pray.
            Today we have cooked [a feast] for so-and-so,
            Today we have given him meat;
            Let the people have good health.

ASSEMBLY: Let the people have good health.

LEADER: Lions and leopards, let them be killed;

ASSEMBLY: Be killed; be killed; be killed;

LEADER: Spears let them be sharp;

ASSEMBLY: Sharp, sharp, sharp.

LEADER: Let the women have good childbirth;

ASSEMBLY: Good, good, good.

LEADER: May food crops germinate,
            May crops ripen;

ASSEMBLY: Ripen, ripen, ripen.

LEADER: Evil things that are in the homestead,
            The setting sun, let it take;

ASSEMBLY: Let it take.
            The setting sun has taken them,
            It has taken them.

151 Invitation to the spirits to lick blood[2]

Spirits, you may walk quickly, you may come and make your clan
happy; if the other spirits are laughing at you you may pooh-pooh
    them [for] they are poor;
you may come, you may lick your blood, it is here.

Timbo, Songwa, Nandoli, Murembe, you may walk quickly;
your cow is here,
you may make [take it] in the belly.

152 Petition uttered to the spirit after death[3]

Thy home is not here with human beings; it is with the beasts;
Leopards await thee; their young require a nature like thine;
Away to thine own, and let them welcome thee!

There is a babe born in this thy village, and there are babes about to
be born: choose for thyself. But be not hasty in choice, for soon
there may be a child in the household of the chief; but whatever
your choice we shall be satisfied: for the babe you choose will become
a person of honour and of good report.

Before thee lie many paths: choose the one most fit for thee to
travel: if it leads thee to what is distasteful, bear with patience thy
lot: if to what is pleasing, remember thy responsibility: thy strength
will be meted to thy need.

The helpless are at thy feet: remember that innocence merits the
gift of simplicity, and weakness should invite strength and sound-
ness: remember also that craft should couple with cruelty and
subtlety with savagery: thine is the choice and thine is the power
and thou wilt go as the spirits intended, but go in peace, and
remember mercy.

153 Sacrificial prayer for the living dead[4]

Let the meat not stick in your throats;
Eat, you chiefs, you ancestor spirits.

They are coming [the oxen]; they see me, whilst I mourn you my
father and my mother, whilst I remain outside, where I receive life
from you, who are below; I remain, I am a miserable wretch. The
oxen are slain; slay the oxen; here they ate. I mourn you. Let us eat
them together, you father and mother. Give me life and give it also
to my children. Let us eat these oxen which I possess, but I possess
them for you. Let us not suffer from complaints of the chest here in
our home.

This is the song by which we accompany you as you return below.
Let us remain in good health.

154 'Living dead: be good to us'[5]

I offer thee this *dege*, this *d'lo* [nuts], and this chicken, in the sacrifice
that I carry out in my name and in the name of my children.

Keep us safe from the *suba* [witches], from all evil and ugly spirits.
Be good to us, keep us from sickness, give us women, healthy
children, and take care to send us rain; give us physical vigour, and
in all ways preserve us that we may gather a bountiful crop.

155 If spirits do not improve they will be forgotten[6]

When have we ever forgotten to make sacrifices to you and to
enumerate your honourable names? Why are you so miserly? If you
do not improve, we will let all your honourable names fall into
oblivion. What will your fate be then! You will have to go and feed
on locusts. Improve: else we will forget you. For whose good is it
that we make sacrifices and celebrate the praises? You bring us
neither harvests nor abundant herds. You show no gratitude
whatever for all the trouble we take. However, we do not wish to
estrange ourselves completely from you and we will say to other men
that we do not completely possess the spirits of our forebears. You
will suffer from it. We are angry with you.

156 Spirits, be patient[7]

Keep me in life and grant me health. O what else must I do, in your
opinion? Have patience: I wish to cut grain until I have earned a
goat to offer up to you. If you hinder me in any way, will you then
perhaps receive anything? Never. And your companions will make
fun of you. Therefore, watch over me and you will receive your due.

KEEPING AWAY THE SPIRITS

157 To persuade a spirit to leave[8]

Come and go with yours—
This is your goat—
This is your road—
Go and don't return.

158 Driving away an unwanted spirit[9]

You, spirit, you must leave this person alone, and you must leave
this village. Come; I will take you to your own body. Come with me.

159 At the digging up of a witch[10]

At the place where the witch was buried the medicine-man sings:

O owl that cries in the thicket. *Fwi! Fwi!*
Oh, come and take away my sorrow.

O spirit, today I'll take you away away.
Come up, come out, I command you.

160 At the digging up of a witch (cont'd)

After digging up the witch's skeleton, they burn it, and the medicine-man smears red paint on his body and sings:

She is showing her teeth in the skull. You weren't burnt in the hole,
Now you're burnt in the hole,
You who showed your teeth in the skull.

161 Separating spirits from a dead body[11]

Your hammock-man was always devoted to you. Each time he called me it was to give you food, to give you renewed strength, because it is you who are the guardian of the earth from which he was moulded. This earth you have allowed to fall to the ground, and since without him you will no longer have work, we the diviners, come today to drive you away from the soul whose destiny you ruled. You will no longer be respected. The body you watched over has been killed. You, too, will be killed today.

162 The diviner next addresses the spirit within as follows:

I kneel before thee, O King, Destroyer—of—all things,
Who—eats—and—leaves—the mouth—soiled.
Thou—of—the thick—lips, *Djokoli kita*,
(Amazfo, Gbogwino Vosu Volo Vodo).

163 Exorcism of spirits[12]

Help me, you spirits of the Ngoni. I have received from your hands this medicine; therefore they must come forth at once from my sick one.

If by chance he has swallowed a snake or a toad that hinders the spirits from coming forth, compel these animals to flee so that there can be a way for the ghosts to depart.

164 For making the talking drum[13]

Spirit of the cedar tree,
The divine drummer announces that,
Had he gone elsewhere (in sleep),
He has now made himself to arise,
As the cock crowed in the early dawn.
We are addressing you, and you will understand.

165 For making the talking drum (cont'd)

Spirit of the mighty one [Elephant],
He and the drummers will return together,
You of mighty bulk, Gyaanadu, the red one,
The swamps swallow thee up, O Elephant,
Elephant that breaks the axe.
Spirit of the Elephant,
The divine drummer announces that
He has started up from his sleep,
He has made himself to arise;
We are addressing you,
And you will understand.

166 To the earth[14]

Earth, while I am yet alive,
It is upon you that I put my trust,
Earth who receives my body.
We are addressing you,
And you will understand.

9 *Rain*

Rain is the symbol of life itself, and the epitome of well-being for people, animals and plants. Rain is for the life of man what health is for the individual. Without sufficient rain the people suffer agony and may ultimately starve; without good health the individual suffers pain and dies. Just as we saw many prayers for healing and good health in chapter 3, we have here a collection of prayers and litanies for rain and good supplies of food. Whereas prayers for healing are made on a personal or family basis in most cases, the ones for rain are made on a community basis since there is nothing like a private supply of rain. When there is a shortage of rain, the whole community suffers: humans, animals and plants. Prolonged droughts are responsible for shortage of food, famines, and large-scale migration of people and livestock.

Prayers 167 to 178 express one wish in common: that God will give people rain. 167 is a communal litany revolving around the benefits of good supply of rain: ripe food, happy women, singing young men, rejoicing old people and overflowing granaries. These benefits constitute people's joy, and they express their expectations with the formula: 'It is well!' Well-being comes with rain.

Prayers 168, 169 and 178 are made together with sacrifices for rain. 'We make this sacrifice in order to have rain.' And people prostrate themselves before God, repeating (168), 'Thou art our Father. Grant us rain.' They fear that they have done something wrong before God which has caused the rain to be withheld. They fear that if they engage in strife and shed one another's blood, 'we will not have rain'. In this prayer the supply of rain is clearly connected with people's moral life, just as it is connected with their physical life. In 169 both the sacrifice and the people's 'wish for rain' are simultaneously presented to Mulungu (God). Other elements of prosperity (e.g. wives, cattle, and goats) depend completely on the supply of rain.

Prayer 170 is the shortest in the whole collection, being only one line (cf. 5, 93 and 217), yet it is very meaningful and effective. In this prayer, rain and God are identified. The presence of God among his people is recognizable through a continuing supply of rain. When it rains, God is in effect 'falling' among the people. This is dynamic symbolism which indicates how much life and its sustenance depend on the rain which is the presence of God himself. It is known that the Ila who offer this prayer refrain for a few days from digging the ground when the new rain season starts, as an act of reverence to God who is represented by the rain.

Rain and prosperity (fatness) are synonymous, according to prayer 171. People complain or affirm, in 172, that 'the Man on high sends no rain'. So they must 'cry out for rain'. Again this prayer clearly links God with rain, and people believe that pleading with him or crying out to him will help to produce the needed rain. Those who offer prayer 174 are rather afraid that they may not get sufficient supply of rain: 'We do not know if God is showering us with blessings or if it is his wish instead to chastise the people.' In their uncertainties they can only affirm that 'up there the Father knows'.

Only God knows whether the rains in a given season will be enough to give a good harvest. Sometimes the rains stop when the crops are too young to bear fruits, and this in reality means punishment or chastisement because people will have worked in vain in their fields and will be faced with famine until the next rains arrive.

The women's and men's litanies (175 and 176) for rain are simple corporate requests. The Masai from whom these two litanies come are chiefly pastoralists. Therefore their main concern here is for a good supply of grass and water. They cry out: 'We need herbs on the earth's back' and 'Quench our thirst!'

Even though, under normal conditions, rain is always very welcome there are occasions when storms endanger people's lives. For this reason, prayers are offered to calm the storms. 179–181 are examples of such prayers. Tropical storms, with thunder and lightning, can be devastating. Prayer 179 is offered under such circumstances: 'Father, thy children are in great anguish. Calm the tempest.' Prayer 180 is offered by the Pygmy people who live by hunting and food-gathering. This particular prayer is used when hunters find themselves caught in the storm while they are in the forest. Under such conditions the rain is a threat to their lives because it brings to an end their hunting expedition, it obliterates the tracks of animals, and makes it very difficult for the hunters to find their way home. So they understandably pray: 'Thy sons are in the forest, Let the rain be slow.' Prayer 181 is another request that the storm be still, the people recalling that a similar storm was instrumental in the death of some known individual.

Rainmaking, as a profession, is fairly widespread in Africa. Some of the prayers for rain would, undoubtedly, be made by rainmakers or other ritual experts. The rainmakers do not in fact make rain, they simply perform the rites which accompany prayers for rain; and they study the weather conditions in order to inform their communities when to expect the new rainy seasons. For that reason, African languages do not refer to them as rainmakers, but use more appropriate terms like 'pointers of rain', 'prayer-makers for rain', and 'askers for rain'. In these prayers it is clear that rain comes from God and it is to him that appeals for rain are directed. For this reason, he is referred to in African societies as the Raingiver, the Watergiver, the Source of Rain, etc. The fact that people think of God as being in the sky or the heavens makes it reasonable to associate him with rain since it falls from the sky. If he were not the God of rain, African peoples would have little to do with him. In the provision of rain lies their chief experience of the love, providence, and the care of God for all people.

PRAYERS FOR RAIN

167 A litany for rain[1]

RECITATIVE:	RESPONSE:
We overcome this wind.	We overcome.
We desire the rain to fall, that it be poured in showers quickly.	Be poured.
Ah, thou rain, I adjure thee fall.	
If thou rainest, it is well.	It is well.
A drizzling confusion.	Confusion.
If it rains and our food ripens, It is well.	It is well.
If the young men sing, it is well.	It is well.
A drizzling confusion.	Confusion.
If our grain ripens, it is well.	It is well.
If our women rejoice,	It is well.
If the children rejoice,	It is well.
If the young men sing.	It is well.
If the aged rejoice,	It is well.
An overflowing in the granary,	Overflowing.
A torrent in flow,	A torrent.
If the wind veers to the south, it is well.	It is well.
If the rain veers to south, it is well.	It is well!

168 At a sacrifice for rain[2]

We make this sacrifice in order to have rain.
If thou hearest our prayer, grant us rain.
Thou art our Father, everyone is here to ask rain of thee.
We are wrong-doers.
If one of us engages in strife today,
If one of us sheds blood, we will not have rain.
Thou art our Father. Grant us rain.
The earth is dry, our families are ruined.
Thou art our Father. Grant us rain.

169 Invocation for rain and wives[3]

Mulungu [God], here is your food.
We wish for rain, for wives, for cattle and for goats to raise;
And we pray God that our people do not die from sickness.

170 For continued rain[4]

Come to us with a continued rain, O Lesa [God], fall!

171 For fatness (rain)[5]

God give us fatness
And we thy people shall be well;
We shall be well with health
That is sweet.

172 Cry for rain[6]

Cry out for rain.
The man on high sends no rain.
Cry out for rain.
He sends no rain.

173 In time of drought[7]

God; have-we-prayed-to-thee,
Give us rain.
Look at this beer and milk.
There is no man who does not bear,
Cover for us pregnant woman of man and ox.

174 'The Father knows'[8]

Torrential rain comes driving down like clubs on the heads of
  people.

And the people say: up there the Father knows.
But we do not know if he is showering us with blessings or if it is
   his wish instead to chastise the people.

175 Women's litany for rain[9]

LEADER: OTHER PEOPLE:

We need herbs on the earth's
back!   Hie! Wae! Almighty God.
The father of Nasira has con-
quered, has conquered.

                                    The highlands and also the low-
                                        lands
                                    Of our vast country which
                                    belongs to thee, O God.
May this be our year, ours in   O messenger of Mbatian's son.
plenty (when you grant us rain!).

176 Men's litany for rain[10]

LEADER: OTHER PEOPLE:

O God of the rain-cloud, hoo-oo!
Quench our thirst!   O God, water us!
                                    Whose powers reach the utter-
                                    most parts of the earth,
                                    hoo-oo!
O God of the black-cloud,
   hoo-oo!   O God, water us!

177 'Let the rain come'[11]

O Tsuni-Goam [God], Father of fathers,
Thou our Father,
Tell Nanub to let the rain come down in torrents,

178 Sacrificial prayer for rain[12]

Tsui-Goab [God], we are now assembled here;
We come to ask for water—
We who are dying from thirst.

PRAYERS TO CALM THE STORM

179 To calm the tempest[13]

Father, thy children are in great anguish.

Calm the tempest, for here live many of thy children.
Seest thou not that we are dying?

180 In the face of a storm[14]

Epilipili [God], Epilipili,
Do not let the rains come.
The rains fall,
The rains come
To burden us with misery.
Thy sons are in the forest;
Let the rain be slow,
Let the rain be slow.

181 Storm: be still![15]

O Aondo [God] of Gbayazge, be still!
It was Aondo of Gbayazge that killed him,
It was he that smote him O!
O Aondo of Gbayazge of Nongov.
Thou Aondo of Gbayazge, be still!

10 *Offerings, sacrifices, and dedications*

Much African religious practice is expressed in the making of offerings and sacrifices. On their own, prayers which accompany a sacrifice do not lend exclusive support to any given theory of the meaning of offerings and sacrifices. They are primarily an expression of the purpose and occasion of the sacrifice, or a request that the spiritual realities accept what is offered or sacrificed.

Six prayers deal with purification. In 182 the people are anticipating their journey to the shrine. They prepare themselves for this by asking the divinity Buk to 'make our country to become clean', probably from disunity. Prayer 183 is intended to remove the social impurities of contracting a marriage between members of the community who otherwise are forbidden to marry. In all African societies there are taboos and sanctions regulating the contracting of marriages. One of the commonest of these is the practice of marrying only someone outside one's own clan provided there are no close kinship ties. The other marriage purification prayer (184) is simply a blessing upon the newly wed couple.

Prayer 185 asks that the home be purified (freed) from enemies and disease. For this purpose, a white herb, vernonia, is waved around while the invocation is pronounced. The rite of sanctifying fire in prayer 186 is performed in connection with the administration of a medical cure. The fire symbolizes the taking (burning) away of the illness. In many societies of the world, fire has the symbolic value of removing impurities. Here it is personified: 'Burn bright, O fire, and take to thyself that which afflicts our brother', so that the sick man 'may be left purged of his affliction'.

Witchcraft is hated in all African societies. There are rituals for cleansing or purifying suspected or certified witches. 187 is an example of the many formulae used at these purification rituals. The purpose is not that God should destroy the witches, but remove their witchcraft so that they are no longer witches. To be a witch is to become an object of hatred and fear in one's community. Once purified of witchcraft, the former witch becomes a normal person acceptable to the community.

In this book the word 'offering(s)' is used to refer to the religious act of presenting items of food (or otherwise) which do not involve the slaughtering of an animal or bird. 'Sacrifice(s)' is used to refer to the presentation of items in which an animal, bird or human being (formerly) is killed for that purpose. (The two terms are also used to refer respectively to the items so presented.) This distinction is not, however, always maintained and our sources use the terms interchangeably. The presentation of offerings and sacrifices is made to God and other spiritual realities.

In prayer 188 incense is burnt either while the hunter is preparing to go into the forest, or while he is actually there. Probably he fears storms, as we saw in the previous chapter; but in any case he wants success, and accordingly appeals to God for it. Sickness calls for libations and offerings of food to the spirits in prayer 189, inviting 'all you spirits of our tribe' to come and eat. Presumably it is feared that the man is sick because the spirits have not been properly fed. If the remedy is made, then his sickness will go away. So, 'come, all of you, to eat this food'. This is the penultimate hope for the cure of the sick.

In prayer 190 we see another address to the spirits, inviting them to accept a chicken. It is not clear whether the chicken has actually been killed. In some offerings, live animals and fowls may be given, and this is probably the case here. The people use the occasion to ask the spirits to 'Shower us with blessings', and defend them from bad spirits. They ask for abundance of food and drink, and good health, sufficient rain and happy families. The offering is simply the context against which the people's needs may be enumerated.

191 accompanies the offering of pieces of meat to the living dead. The deceased father has 'been complaining for meat', so now he gets it and is asked to 'Invite your brothers all: Meat for you is here.' This and other prayers addressed to the departed show how the living feel the reality of the presence of the living dead. Here they speak face to face with the departed, even if the oral communication is only one way. The departed respond by 'eating' and 'drinking' what they have been given, and by granting the requests which accompany such giving. In this prayer, other than simply telling the departed to eat and be satisfied, no specific request is made. In 192, a goat, which had at one time been dedicated to the spirit of a deceased head of the family, needs to be exchanged when it has grown old or has to be killed. This invocation simply puts the exchange in its proper setting. The living dead is supposed to accept

the deal and be satisfied. Milk is offered to the departed in prayer
193, and the deceased head of the family is asked to 'Look after your
family'.

Prayers connected with sacrifices are of a similar pattern to those
which accompany the making of offerings. In most cases they present
the sacrifice before God, and then make known people's requests.
In 194, the meat is presented without any request; presumably,
then, the requests would have been made on another occasion but
without sacrifice.

Prayer 195 opens with a declaration that the people (Chagga)
know God, because he is not a stranger to them since their myth of
creation speaks of God as having caused men to burst out of a vessel.
So they praise him and prostrate before him. Their first request is
that he will receive the bull that they sacrifice to him; then that he
will heal the sick; and thirdly that they will produce children
in large numbers 'like bees'. The prayer ends with a blessing. This
is the common structure of prayers for accompanying offerings and
sacrifices. We see that same structure in prayer 196, in which a
statement of faith or fact is made first, then the presentation of the
sacrifice, 'Today we give you your food', followed by a list of the
requests for good health, wealth, and many children, and ending with
a statement of satisfaction: 'We like to hear the cries of children.'

Prayer 197 has a particular historical setting. It is occasioned by
the visit of a man and his wife from Britain to the homestead of a
leading man (perhaps a chief). As an expression of hospitality, the
man slaughters a sheep for the visitors, and offers it to God together
with beer. This is an expression of joy at welcoming the visitors, and
the corporate sacrifice to God serves to symbolize the unity of the
friendship which is being created on this occasion. The host prays
for good health and safety of the visitors, and for himself that he be
protected from getting 'very ill'. To sacrifice to God is a sacred act
which removes any enmity from those who join in the solemn act.
They are in effect praying with one accord, they are united in the
sacrificial animal, and they express that unity in eating together the
meat of the animal and drinking the beer that remains after offering
a libation to God.

In prayer 198, a man sacrifices to a divinity as an act of committing
himself to the divinity: 'Today, you have completed marriage with
me.' Then he asks that the divinity should 'stand at my back with a
good standing', that is, that it should protect him in his undertakings
and life.

Prayers 199–212 are grouped together under the notion of dedication or consecration. In 199 and 200, a newly born baby is dedicated to God. The intention is to show that children come from God, and are very tender, and to ask God to look after them so that they can grow safely up to maturity. In prayer 199 we appreciate the tenderness with which the parents handle their baby as they dedicate it to God: 'I offer this fresh bud . . . I offer this new plant.' Even the parents consider themselves to be the children of God, needing parental care from him. Similar sentiments are expressed in 200 which opens with words of tenderness: 'Gently! Gently! Here is the child. Let him grow tall.' The prayer is offered by a medicine-man who is here playing the role of the pastor, the priest. He administers some of his medicine, perhaps more for their ritual than physical value, so that a tangible expression of his good will for the baby can be seen by all the people. He acknowledges that the medicines have come from God, and he appeals ultimately to him to do the blessing: 'You gave me these medicines: let them protect the child against sickness. . . .'

As we saw in chapter 7 initiation is a valuable institution in many African societies. Prayer 201 is for the consecration of young people before they undergo circumcision which is the most common initiation for a large number of African communities.

I find prayer 202 difficult to interpret. The word 'ants' is a symbolic figure of speech, referring to the Dinka people. It is an expression of humility, and is commonly used also by the Nuer who are neighbours of the Dinka. The prayer carries a sense of self-dedication or presentation before the divinity or the first human beings. Similarly prayer 203 is a personal dedication to Orisa-nla, the Yoruba divinity, said to be God's deputy on earth in creative and executive functions.

Prayers 204, 205 and 206 are offered to consecrate and bless new homesteads. The intention in the consecration is: 'May we stay with peace' (204), and 'May the person who is going to live in this house have many children . . . may he be safe all these years' (205). Prayer 206 categorically tells us that the storeyed house is not as important as the men who live in it. The beauty of the home is not in the buildings: it is much more in the persons who dwell there. Prayer 211 falls in this category of dedicating a new homestead, except here it is a tree that is planted and blessed for the new home. The tree symbolizes new life growing up there, and its prosperity is mystically transferred to the dwellers of the new home. Therefore the prayer is 'Bless this tree, make it grow . . . Remove all evil, let it not come but let the good come . . .' The prayer goes on to personalize the request, asking for wealth and health and ending with a request, 'Let all blessings abound.'

Prayer 207 is offered by the Ashanti king, to bless (sprinkle) the famous golden stool which symbolizes the history, the kingdom, the prosperity and well-being of the people. The king invokes upon the mystical power of the stool to 'return sharp and fierce', to enable him to continue winning battles as he did formerly. Then he prays for life, for prosperity of his soldiers, for increase of children, for success of the hunters and miners, and for an increase of personal wealth in gold.

Incantations over the new sword (208) and the magic spear (209) are for success whenever the sword and spear are used. The beer-trough is prayed for, in number 210, dedicating it to God under his different attributes. It is hoped that such a dedication will keep away evil from the homestead where it is used: 'Let it not bring any evil thing to this home, Let the beer fermented in it be good, Let it be a good serving-vessel for all who use it.'

Like some of the prayers in the second chapter, prayer 212 dedicates people's life for the new year. Wine and food are offered to mark the end of the year and create the platform for asking 'that at the end of next year we may be able to give you food'. This simply means that the people wish to remain alive up to the end of the new year. Special mention of some eminent people is made, asking for long life for them.

These prayers show people's readiness to give their material possessions, animals, foodstuffs and beverages to spiritual realities. Food and drink have mystical links between man and man, and between man and the spiritual realities. They not only provide nourishment to man, but they also sustain relationships between people and the spiritual realm. Even though man does not, and need not, feed God, when man offers or sacrifices to him, this puts man into a specially close proximity with God. There is also a feeling among many African societies that relationships between people and the living dead can only be renewed and maintained through man's offerings of food and drink. These tokens are symbols of remembrance and welcome, since the departed continue to be present with the living, for a few generations at least.

The acts of dedicating children or new homes to God are indications of people's concern to remain in a harmonious relationship with

God and the spirit realm. In so doing, they recognize that their children and belongings are gifts from God which they give back to him so that he will bless them, ensuring for the children long life and a happy home. The physical world is recognized as interlinking with the spiritual world. As man wants the blessings of the spiritual realm, he in turn gives what is physical to the spiritual. Again we see that man is the priest of nature, soliciting the spiritual for the physical and offering the physical to the spiritual.

PURIFICATION

182 Hymns anticipating a journey to the shrine[1]

We bend our knees to Garang and Kerjok,
Deng of the byre (*luak :* byre or shrine) help me
Father it is you who will let me go through your legs,
You will give us the ashes called Muonylek,

Buk [*Abuk*], mother of *Deng*,
Leave your home in the sky and come to work in our homes.
Make our country to become clean like the original home of *Deng*,
Come make our country as one; the country of Akwol
Is not as one, either by night or by day.
The child called Deng, his face has become sad,
The children of Akwol have bewildered their chief's mind.

Oh we are going to *Deng*
At our ancient byre [shrine].
Let us reach up to the poles of the byre
In our original home. I have put sandals on my feet,
Nyiel is going to his byre.

183 Purifying a forbidden marriage[2]

You have acted with strong determination. Now eat the liver. Eat it in the full light of day, not in the dark! It will be a *mhamba*, an offering to the spirits.

You spirits, look; We have done it in the daylight. It has not been done by stealth. Bless them, give them children.

So be it. They have decided to marry each other; you, spirits of the boy and girl, unite them together so that they do not hate each other; let them not remind each other that they are brother and sister; let their union not be spoilt by such remembrance, nor by other people saying to them: 'You have been guilty of witchcraft. You have married your relative!'

184 Purification of a newly married couple[3]

Tihatlhadinusanen, take the smoke, there it is, take it
right up to the place of Molelale, Molelale chief of the clouds.

185 Purification of the home[4]

This is Vernonia
Let my home be as white as it.
This is Bersama
Let it spare my house.
This is cardiospermum
Keep away my enemies.
These are yours, Creator
And yours, O Giver,
And yours, Lord of the sun.
I wish you give me health.

186 To the purifying fire[5]

Burn, fire: rise sparks: for our brother Lokwerabok lies ill and they
are calling him. Burn red for the life that is in him. Burn bright, O
fire, and take to thyself that which afflicts our brother that, rising
with the smoke, it may vanish as the smoke vanishes, and he may be
left purged of his affliction and whole of the sickness which would
destroy him. By our great ancestors I adjure thee, O fire, that seeing
thee and savouring thy smoke, the smoke which carries our
entreaties, they may be content and grant that our brother remain.

187 Song of purification of a witch[6]

The older person is the Creator (he finds out)
Here they are, those who totter (the witches)
Why don't you do away with the witch who stands in the middle of
the village?
Glory to the Creator.

OFFERINGS

188 At the offering of incense[7]

Grandfather [God], Great Father,
Let matters go well with me,
For I am going into the forest to hunt.

If already in the forest:
Father, thy children are afraid,
Behold: we shall die!

189 Invitation to all the spirits[8]

Here is our food. All you spirits of our tribe, invite each other. I do
not say that you are jealous, but you who have raised this sick man,
summon all the spirits.
Come, all of you, to eat this food.

190 An offering of a secret society[9]

N'tomo yea, see this chicken, a beautiful chicken, no?
N'tomo, in all our names, I offer thee this chicken as a sacrifice.
   Shower us with blessings, defend us from the furious genii of
the thorn-brakes and from bad spirits. Make us strong and vigorous.
Send us an abundance of food and drink, keep us safe from sickness.
Give us rains and good crops, O N'tomo, and bless us with happy
families

191 Invocation of presenting meat to the living dead[10]

Father, you have been complaining for meat.
Meat today here it is
Come and partake of it:
Invite your brothers all:
Meat for you is here.

The ancestor, today he has spoken.
Bring forth billy goat brown, chicken, and beer

Father, you have been complaining for meat.
Meat today here it is
Come and partake of it:
Invite your brothers all:
Meat for you is here!

192 Invocation for exchanging a goat for the departed[11]

I have taken away your goat.
See, I have placed another one for you.

193 Offering milk to the departed[12]

Receive your cow's milk
Look after your family
Defend your children against dangers.
Look after your property in this home.

SACRIFICES

194 Invocation of offering meat to God[13]

This is yours the Giver [Rugaba],
And this is yours the Creator [Rubanga],
And this is yours the Sunlike [Kazooba].

195 Sacrificial prayer facing Mt Kilimanjaro[14]

We know thee, God, Chief, Preserver,
He who burst forth men that they lived.
We praise thee, and pray to thee, and fall before thee.
Chief, receive this bull of thy name,
Heal him to whom thou gavest it and his children.
Sow the seed of offspring with us,
That we may beget like bees.
Now, Chief, Preserver, bless all that is ours.

196 'We like to hear the cries of children'[15]

You elders, Okango, Olapa [and other names],
Today we give you your food,
Give us health and wealth,
Let all bad things go with the setting sun,
Let them go afar.
Spirits, our homestead is now silent:
Give our women children,
We like to hear the cries of children.

197 At a sacrifice to express hospitality[16]

O God, accept this njohi [beer], for the white man has come to my homestead. If the white man becomes ill let him not be very ill nor his wife. The white man has come from his home through the waters; he is a good man; the people who work for him he treats well; let them not argue with him. If the white man and his wife get ill, let them not be very ill because I and the white man unite in sacrifice to you. Let him not die, because to you we sacrifice an excellent fat ram. The white man has come from afar to us, and has made an agreement with me to sacrifice to you. Wherever he may go let him not be very ill, because he is good and is exceedingly well-off, and I also am good and rich, and I and the white man are even as of one mother. God, a big sheep have I dedicated. The white man and his wife, and I and my people go to sacrifice a sheep at the foot of a tree—a most

valuable sheep. Let me not be very ill, for I have taught him how to
sacrifice to you even as an M'Kikuyu.

198 Sacrificing to a divinity[17]

Divinity [obosom] so-and-so, accept this sheep and eat;
today you have completed marriage with me; this is a sheep
from my hands, stand at my back with a good standing.

DEDICATION AND CONSECRATION

199 Dedicating a baby to God[18]

To thee, the Creator, to thee, the Powerful,
I offer this fresh bud,
New fruit of the ancient tree.
Thou art the master, we thy children.
To thee, the Creator, to thee, the Powerful,
Khmvoum [God], Khmvoum,
I offer this new plant.

200 Presentation of a child[19]

Abousaye [gently]! *Akhwari* [sweetly]! Here is the child.
Let him grow tall, let him grow into manhood with your medicines.
Let his sweat be pure, let the stains go, let them go to Chibouri, let
them go to Nkhabelane! Let the child play happily, let him be like
his friends. This is not my first try. You gave me these medicines:
let them protect the child against sickness so that no one can say
they are powerless.

201 Consecration before circumcision[20]

The child is going into the bush, Altar, receive your water and wood:
Let not the good power depart with the blood!
Let the evil power depart!

202 Hymn of self-presentation[21]

I will cut off the tongues of ants
But spare their ears.
Speech of the ants keeps silence.
I will cut off the tongues of ants
But spare their ears.
Awok descends upon the cattle hut
The cattle hut of Daiyim,

Abuk descends upon the cattle hut
The cattle hut of Daiyim,
Garang descends upon the cattle hut
The cattle hut of Daiyim.
Here are my words of Daiyim
Here is my speech of Daiyim.

203 Commitment to service[22]

He who makes eyes, makes nose,
It is the Orisa I will serve;
He who makes one as he chooses,
It is the Orisa I will serve;
He who sends me here,
It is the Orisa I will serve.

204 Consecration of a new house[23]

May we stay well in this country; we did not know that we would
arrive here. May we stay with peace and dream honey [i.e., have
pleasant dreams]; the God of old, the sun, when it rises in the east.
may it bring us honey, and when it goes to set in the west may it take
the badness with it.

205 Blessing a new house[24]

May the person who is going to live in this house have many
children; may he be rich; may he be honest to the people and good to
the poor; may he not suffer from disease or any other kind of
trouble; may he be safe all these years.

206 Ceremony of the 'storeyed house'[25]

They say the houses of Molu in Tombeke are fine,
That the houses of Molu are fine.
In Molu the houses have storeys.
But it is the men who are fine,
Not the storeyed houses!

207 Sprinkling the golden stool[26]

Friday, Stool of Kings, I sprinkle water upon you,
may your power return sharp and fierce.
Grant that when I and another meet (in battle), grant it be as when
    I met Denkyira; you let me cut off his head.
As when I met Akyem; you let me cut off his head.

As when I met Domma; you let me cut off his head.
As when I met Tekiman; you let me cut off his head.
As when I met Gyman; you let me cut off his head.
The edges of the years have met.
I pray you for life.
May the warriors prosper.
May the hunters kill meat.
May the women bear children.
We who dig for gold, let us get gold to dig,
And grant that I get some for the upkeep of my kingship.

208 Incantation over a new sword[27]

If the owner of this meets with an enemy, may you go straight and kill your adversary; but if you are launched at one who has no evil in his heart, may you miss him and pass on either side without entering into his body.

209 Prayer over the magic spear[28]

Thou hast brought us here to help us.
Tomorrow we must fight: none of us shall fall, but only the enemy.
If one of us is wounded, let it not be to the death, but so that he can
    be borne home.
With thee let it be granted to us to recover our wives and children
    that are taken prisoner by the enemy.

210 Dedicating the beer-trough to God[29]

I am going to have a beer-trough made,
The beer-trough is yours, Kazooba [the Shining One];
The beer-trough is yours, Rugaba [the Giver];
The beer-trough is yours, Nyamuhanga [the Creator].

Let this trough be made well,
Let it not bring any evil thing to this home,
Let the beer fermented in it be good,
Let it be a good serving-vessel for all those who use it.

211 Dedicating a new homestead[30]

Bless this tree, make it grow, let it be entirely a blessing without any evil. Remove all evil, let it not come but let only the good come. Give thy blessing that we may increase in all things and grow wealthy and be free from disease. Let blessings abound.

212 Dedicating life for the new year[31]

Esu kese Afu, come and take your wine.

We have reached the end of the year, here is your wine,
   come and take it, here is your food, here also is your fowl,
   give us life and strength.

Give us strength so that at the end of next year we may be able to
   give you food. Life to Kwesi Enim; life to the European; life to
   the Chief, and life to Abenase.

11 *Confidence, confession, and creed*

A large number of prayers proclaim man's belief and confidence in God, or what they believe about him. In this chapter we have 38 prayers covering a wide range of related beliefs: that God listens to man's prayers, a confession of confidence and trust in God, an assurance of his spiritual aid, of man's humility as he approaches God and a credal declaration of his religious beliefs.

Prayers 213–217 carry the idea that God listens to people, and they should continue to call upon him. In 213, God's attention is drawn by asking him to 'Listen to us, aged God. . . . Look at us, everlasting God.' To call him aged simply means that he endures for ever, he has always been. The people are in desperation and tell him that he may take their beautiful women, slaves and horses, if he wants them. They would do anything for God, if only he will listen to their prayers. Prayer 214 calls upon the people to 'turn again to the real God'. It blames, by implication, the ruination of the country upon people's failure to pray to God. He is ready to protect and look after their country—if only they would turn to him and pray.

In prayer 215, the national founder of the Shilluk is called upon to plead for his people before God so that he may grant rain to them. This is one of the very few prayers involving a national intermediary between God and men. Yet the Shilluk do also pray directly to God, even though they treat Nyikang as an intermediary to whom they sometimes address their prayers as well. A similar idea occurs in prayer 216, in which Longar, 'first created by the Creator', is asked not to cease praying, for 'The Creator will listen, he who created Longar in the past.' So Longar acts in the capacity of an intermediary, though his position is not as clearly defined as that of Nyikang in the previous prayer. The people seem to put the burden of praying upon themselves when they declare that 'If Pagong pray, God the great One is brought to the country.'

Prayer generally assumes that the person praying has confidence and trust in God (or whoever the object of the prayer may be). Some of the prayers in this collection specifically mention the confidence and trust which individuals and communities have in

God, not only in the moment of praying, but also in their life as a whole. In prayer 218, the person declares confidently that even if the entire tribe should fight against him, 'I shall not fear'. This prayer expresses complete confidence in God, which is similar to that of Psalm 23. The same note is sounded in the next prayer (219), in which the person says: 'I can do everything' even if 'all the people hate (me).' Whatever threatens him he is sure that his guardian divinity ('Flesh of my father') will defend him and drive it away.

Prayer 220 is a hymn which declares people's religious belief. It begins with an acknowledgement that people's words have angered God and he 'has turned his back on us'. But the people have the faith that God will yet turn about, and listen to them and help them. They know that: 'We are the children of our Maker. And do not fear that he will kill us.' This indicates their belief that God will forgive them and spare their lives. Even 'in the time of privation', when death threatens because men have angered God, one's confidence in God inspires hope: 'In the time of privation I will not fear.' The reason for all this is that one has 'prayed and prayed'. Consequently God's faithfulness will remain and he will keep the people safe and secure.

This prayer lifts the life of man from the level of despondence to the great heights of spiritual confidence and faith in God. God remains true, loving, ever ready to forgive and help the people who are his children. Even when troubles arise, one faces them with an invincible confidence that God will 'ever keep' one safe. The more one prays the stronger grows one's faith in the goodness of God.

Prayer 221 is made at the making of a sacrifice. It opens with a declaration of belief in God as the only Creator. In his sight everyone is precious, nobody is odious. The appeal is then made to God the merciful, to spare the life of those whom he has created, since none is powerful in the sight of God. Man has come before God in great humility: 'I have paid the price' (of sacrificing an ox). Now man appeals to God to let the sick live. God is the ultimate source of life, and appeal is made to him in that.

Prayers 222 and 223 declare categorically that people pray only to God. Their trust in him is total. He is 'The God who thunders and it rains'; 'To thee only I pray.' These statements do away with any other sources of spiritual help. They are monotheistic, since every day one prays only to him. In 223, the person concerned tells us that he has made up his mind and has 'taken God to me'. As a result, his enemies dare not attack him. To take God to oneself in

faith is to take the ultimate shield against all enemies. It is to commit
oneself to God the protector. This prayer has a personal application
in an otherwise communally held belief in God. It declares in effect
that one has been 'converted' from corporate to personal realiza-
tion of, or belief in, God which is the basic tenet of African religious
belief. This personal belief in God also comes out in prayer 225:
'In thy greatness, I am great and agree to thy will.'

In this prayer God is described in maternal terms whereas in the
majority of the prayers he is depicted as masculine. Here she is
'Mother of men, Mother of beasts', indicating that she is their source
of life, their Creator, their Maker, their Mother who not only makes
them but feeds them, nourishes them, protects them, gives truly and
generously to them.

In prayers 226–230, we see a kind of assurance which people keep
in mind while praying. For this reason, they encourage one another
to pray: 'Let us lift our voices in prayer. . . . The Creator of the
sky gives us peace, Gives us food' (226). The people pray in an
assurance that God listens, accepts their offerings or sacrifices,
and gives them what they need most (food and peace). Only in a
peaceful relationship with God do people 'gain good health'; and
this relationship is generated through prayer and offerings to the
Creator. In prayer 227, man sacrifices a goat and pleads that God
will turn his eyes and cure the sick. Prayers and sacrifices are the
final means of moving the powers: 'Grant my prayer, O king, O
heaven, let yourself be moved.' When the request has been granted,
God is not forgotten: rather does one promise to make another
sacrifice. Man's relationship with God is not a one-way affair in
which man only asks and receives from God; man also gives to God,
and the sacrifice is the greatest gift that man can offer to his Creator.
In this exchange, man is assured of God's response by receiving the
sacrifice or offering, listening to man's prayers, and answering the
requests of man.

Man feels terribly lonely if spiritual realities forsake him. In
prayer 228, someone argues with the divinity Flesh that if he
forsakes him, he will stop sacrificing or making offerings to him:
'If I am forsaken by it, I shall give no more.' He is concerned about
those who love him and those who hate him. Similarly in prayer 229,
the Dinka is searching for the divinities Deng and Dengdit, and calls
out for them: 'Where art thou gone?' These divinities give an
assurance that there is no vacuum in the spiritual structure, particularly in the area between man and God. The agony caused by such

a vacuum is revealed when the man prays that he may not be abandoned or thrust 'into the arms of the malign spirit'. He wants assurance that his guardian divinities are present, and that they will 'Come . . . with a gift from the man on high. The gift is from God.' When the spiritual realities seem to be eclipsed and man cannot reach them, man suffers the agony of spiritual abandonment.

The national prayer (230) of the Shilluk is full of religious meaning. God is implored and it is only to him that one prays. He is the One who sustains people all the time; and he is omnipresent, for 'I walk with thee: when I sleep in the night, I sleep with thee.' God is providential, and supplies people with food and water which constitute their sustenance. It is he who keeps people alive not only in this but also in the next life: 'The soul is kept alive by thee.' The prayer acknowledges God to be supreme: 'There is no one above thee, thou God.' Then it moves into Shilluk mythology, to point out the belief that God made Nyikang and all mankind, thus becoming 'the grandfather of Nyikang (and) man'.

On the question of calamities and national distress, God is ultimately involved: 'If a famine comes, is it not given by Thee?' The cow which is about to be sacrificed belongs to God both when it is alive and when dead. God is the ultimate point of reference for the people: 'Thou God, to whom shall we pray, is it not to thee?' God is the goal of spiritual turning; and even the soul (spirit) of man itself belongs to God. An immediate application of the prayer is an acknowledgement that God is the One who raises up the sick, helps the needy, and saves those who are in danger or other trouble.

Prayer 231 like 226, is a call to prayer: 'O men and children, come along, pray to God!' Man must humble himself before God. His presence is recognized; it cannot be evaded because it pursues 'us over his wide plains'. The prayer does not, however, indicate how that presence is recognized except, perhaps, through belief and confidence. Indeed the people feel so sure about God's presence that they summon one another, both young and old, to 'Pray to our God'. The man who utters prayer 232 is in misery. Therefore he invokes God to help him, regarding himself to be like an ant. He reminds God: 'Alas, I am your child.' Therefore he prays in the confidence of a child, speaking to his Father.

In prayers 233 to 238 we get a rare element in African prayers, the confession of wrongdoing, the request for forgiveness, and the purification or absolution. In 233 and 234, a man declares before

God that his son whom he begat and trained refuses to do some work for him. The man pronounces a formal curse on his disobedient son, and leaves the matter there until his son returns and asks for forgiveness. Some time goes by, and in the words of prayer 234, his son returns home, much like in the parable of the prodigal son (Luke 15.11–25), and begs his father to remove the curse. The father prays for forgiveness and prosperity for his now-repentant son so that 'Wherever he goes now may he prosper and have many children.' In these two prayers, it is the father who actually 'confesses' to God that his son has wronged him, and it is the father who also declares forgiveness or absolution for his son. We know only indirectly that his son has repented, probably not so much of his wrongdoing as of the misery he has suffered through the curse of his father. The fear of the formal curse is great in African societies, and nobody can remain confortable as long as a curse invoked by his parents, aunt, uncle or other close relative lingers in his mind.

The leader who recites prayer 235 asks for God's forgiveness on behalf of a offender. It is not the offender's prayer. Other members of the community join in the response asking for rain or other communal benefits. It is possible that someone in the community has broken a serious taboo which is thought to have caused the national calamity (in this case drought). Therefore, this breach has to be healed and God is asked to forgive.

Thunder and lightning can be frightening phenomena in the tropics. In prayer 236, it is feared that lighting might strike, therefore one prays to God, declaring that one is not deserving of death by lightning. Even if one is innocent, one prays nevertheless to be left alone (be forgiven). In this case God is associated with thunder, he is manifested in it, it is his voice and a powerful voice at that.

An interesting form of confession and forgiveness occurs in prayer 237 which is in two parts. Part (a) is a declaration of offence committed by someone who kills or eats the sacred animal (ntana). It is not the offender who confesses the matter to God: this is done by the medicine-man to whom he has revealed the matter. The priest or medicine-man declares that any misfortunes that may befall the man will be consequent upon his having killed the sacred animal. The medicine-man prays, however, that the offender may be healed. It is the normal practice that when a person goes to the medicine-man for treatment, he has to speak freely about what he has done, in order that the mystical causes of his sickness may be established. In this case the patient confesses having killed the tabooed animal. In the second part of the prayer, (b), the patient himself prays for forgiveness, confessing that he has violated the taboo. He offers food to God and prays: 'Grant me peace. Forgive me. Grant me a happy end. Deliver me from bad sickness, deliver me from suffering.' Here forgiveness is tantamount to peace of the mind and the body. Forgiveness is to be experienced through the cure of his disease and relief from suffering.

Prayer 238 is for the absolution of moral offenders. Their immorality must be thoroughly removed, before there is peace and tranquillity in the community. It has to be erased and buried: 'Carry it to the spirit in the mountain. Put it in a deep pit; place a stone upon it. . . .' God is able to accomplish such a forgiveness. An offering is made at the same time, indicating people's desires to be fully protected from the consequences of the offence.

Prayers 239 to 250 introduce several articulations of African traditional proto-creeds. Prayer 239 confesses God to be Father, Creator, giver of life, and to draw nigh when a sacrifice is made to him. The individual, possibly on behalf of himself and others, is resolute about turning to God, invoking God, praying to God, and asking God to give life. He calls upon God to come. 'To thee, my God, I turn. . . . O Father, Creator, come!' In the act of sacrifice, God 'comes' to be present with the people, to receive their sacrifice, to listen to their prayers, and to give them life (just as they give him the life of the animal). At this moment of worship, God is united with his people—he comes to them, just as they have come to him; as they are united with one another on the horizontal level, now they wish to be united with God on the vertical level.

This is a moment of great spiritual elevation: 'O Father, come; How can I reconcile myself with thee?' In this rhetorical question, man recognizes himself as falling short of the spiritual heights where God would come and man would meet him. But the prayer shows, among other things, that he is God who meets people, and that people experience this meeting at the moment of worship, at the act of sacrificing to him and calling upon him.

Prayer 240 simply proclaims that this is God's universe, and that God's will prevails in it. The people proclaim God to be 'our Father', and ask him to 'remove all evil from our path'. Evil is to be understood here primarily in physical terms—diseases, drought, ill health, failures, misfortunes and the like. Prayer 241 makes no special request to God: it simply reports people's belief that God is present in the bush (i.e. always, since the bush is ever present in their country). He is also the God who was, who is and who has no ending.

The declaration made in prayer 242 simply sets God in his transcendence, over against man's very limited state: 'Nzame (God) is Nzame, Man is Man.' The nature of God is entirely other, and there is an unbridgeable gap between him (in his nature) and man: 'Each to himself, each in his dwelling.' Prayer 243 tells that God is the creator of people, and has given them 'the capacity to feel hunger. So we need grain. . . .' It is logical to ask God to feed the people whom he has created since it is he who has given them capacity for hunger.

Prayer 244 is a summary of God's initial creative activity. It is not unlike chapter 1 of the book of Genesis, even if more brief. It is a magnificent song of creation and the mortality of mankind. 'In the time when God created all things, He created the sun. And the sun is born and dies and comes again. . . . He created man. And man is born and dies and comes not again.' There lies both the beauty of creation and the tragedy of death in human life.

In prayer 245 we see the transcendence of God contrasted with his immanence. God is both far off and near; yet he is invisible so that even when he is near he cannot be seen ('he is not here').

It is unusual, in African religious heritage, to find God presented as speaking to man (except in mythological settings). In prayer 246 reference is made to such communication of God to men: 'Thus speaketh the Creator of men, But the men refuse to listen. On us shall descend some awful curse.' But the prayer does not tell us what God is saying, only that people disobey and consequently it is feared that he will punish them severely with a devastating curse as in former times. The prayer does not tell us what God's voice is, only to complain that certain men do not know it and will not get anything from the Father. The prayer is set in a family situation, in which the disobedient children are cursed by their father (mother or other close relative), and do not know (listen to) the voice of their father. As in a human family, God 'is the one who loves man'. So also in the spiritual setting, men as the children of God fail to listen, to obey the voice of God, and he lets some calamity, or other form of curse, descend upon them; yet he still loves them. This prayer sets the tenderness of God's love over against the repeated disobedience of man.

Prayers 247 to 250 constitute what we might really call African creeds, declarations of people's faith as it were. Prayer 247 revolves around the concept of God who was in the beginning, is there today and will be there tomorrow and forever. He is truly everlasting, spanning the three dimensions of a linear concept of time. Futhermore, he is spirit, therefore he cannot be represented pictorially since 'he has no body'. God is metaphorically like a spoken word: 'That word! It is no more, It is past and still it lives! So is God.'

Prayers 248 and 249 are statements of faith concerning the concept of existence. 'The source of being is above.' God is the source of existence, he gives life to men, and protects them from perishing through famine. Prayer 249 categorically affirms that 'all our lives depend' on God of our forefathers, 'and without you we are nothing.' Man without God is nothing, he cannot exist, he cannot live, he cannot prosper, he cannot be man. 'Without you we can't live. . . . You are the source of life.' The prayer goes on to recall that people do not know their historical origins, but God does. He is also seen as 'the God of wars and fights', through whose help people have survived. Therefore, they now ask for continued protection especially on the family basis. They present God with a sacrifice or offering, to show their complete commitment to him and their sincerity before him.

In prayer 250 we hear an African statement of what a true human being is. A true human being has a religious foundation: he knows how to perform rites, he knows what is profane and how to keep away from it, he knows that sacrificing and praying to God will produce results, even the results of bearing children and causing it to rain. In short, then, a genuine Mukamba, African or human being, is a religious person and anyone who falls short of this religious grounding is not a whole human being.

The prayers in the latter part of this chapter take us deep into African traditional spirituality. Man puts his absolute trust in God; man confesses God to be God and he himself to be a creature dependent upon God. Man recognizes that a relationship between him and God is possible, and that God responds to and respects that relationship whose ongoing existence depends so much on man himself.

ASSURANCE

213 Listen to us, O God[1]

Listen to us, aged God,
Listen to us, everlasting God who has ears!

Look at us, aged God,
Look at us, everlasting God who has eyes!
Receive us, ancient God,
Receive us, everlasting God who has hands!
If you love beautiful horses, take them!
If you love beautiful women, take them!
If you love beautiful slaves, take them!
Listen to us, O God,
O God, listen to us.

214 Why not turn again to God?[2]

O Shilluk, cause of the ruination of our lands;
Why not turn again to God, up there?
Why not turn again to the real God?

To God the protector who looks after the country?
To God the giver who looks after the country?

215 'Call upon God'[3]

I call upon Grandfather Nyikang,
I spread the palms of my hands in prayer:
O Nyikang, implore God, who hath created the earth.

Nyikang, call upon God,
for he has created men,
for he sends forth the rain.

O sharpener of spears, little Yelo,
call upon God,
Who has generated men,
until he grants rain to Nyikang, sharpener of spears.

216 The Creator will listen[4]

It was great Longar, first created by the Creator,
And Jiel of the *awar* grass, first created
Shrines and fishing-spears and the *alal* spear
And prayer and invocation.
Do not cease to pray, do not cease Longar,
The child of the warrior clan cannot head the camp,
You will be married into the camp.
The warrior clans cannot head the camp,
You will be married into the camp.
The warrior clans cannot head the camp

If masters of the fishing-spear and Divinity do not help the land;
Yet the Creator will listen, he who created Longar in the past.
If it be war, then we shall ask Pagong, all Pagong,
Pagong of the Awan tribe, Pagong of the Wau tribe.
In the subtribe Biong, do not Pagong lead there?
Great master of the *alal* spear,
If Pagong pray, God the great One is brought to the country.

217 God is always ready to be entreated[5]

O Ruwa [God] protect me and mine!

218 'I shall not fear'[6]

Though the tribe holds a feast against me
I shall not fear,
Though all the pople hold a feast against me
I shall not fear,
O my tribe, I am a bull with sharpened horns,
I am a maddened bull.

219 'I can do everything'[7]

On my landing-place at Gutacol
I can do everything
And all the people hate [me].
Flesh [one of the divinities] of my father is like the flanks of an army:
It protects me on all sides, scattering [enemies].
Flesh of my father is drawn out of the river [Nile]
Scattering enemies on all sides.
What comes unseen from behind, it drives away,
What strikes me in the eye, it drives away.
It is driven away, my red father [Flesh],
Flesh of my father scatters them.

CONFIDENCE AND TRUST

220 'We are the children of God'[8]

God has turned his back on us;
The words of men have made him wrathful.
And yet he will turn about again.
God has turned his back on us.

We are the children of our Maker
And do not fear that he will kill us.

We are the children of God
And do not fear that he will kill.

How, in the time of privation,
Will the people live?
In the time of privation
I will not fear.
Because I have prayed and prayed,
The word of the Lord will not be mocked,
His good word will ever keep thee.

221 'O merciful God, turn thine eyes'[9]

O Nhialic [God] thou alone generated them,
Thou alone made them.
No one finds them odious.
Oh merciful Nhialic, turn thine eyes upon life.
No one is powerful.
Accept this ox.
I have paid the price.
Now let them live.

222 God to whom I pray[10]

LEADER: GROUP RESPONSE:

My God, to thee alone I pray,
The God who thunders and it rains:
Give me an offspring!   Every day,
                                           To thee only I pray.

O Morning Star that rises forth   Every day,
                                           To thee only I pray.

He who is like a sage,
To whom I offer my prayer.   Every day,
                                           To thee only I pray.

O God, to whom prayer is made,
The God who hears our prayer.   Every day,
                                           To thee only I pray.

223 'I have taken God to me'[11]

I pray to Juok, God the giver, God the protector, I have taken
God to me and have become fearful to my enemies, so that they
scarcely dare attack me.

224 'I have come to shave your head'[12]

I pray to Thee, Jouk [God],
I have come to shave your head [i.e. cut down the vegetation].
Let me dwell in peace,
let the grain ripen;
let no harm come to me when I cut the trees.
Now I have paid the price by killing a goat.
Let me remain happy.

225 'In thy greatness, I am great'[13]

O Mawu Sodza [God] Mother of men, Mother of beasts. If thou givest to man, thou givest truly. If thou deniest to man, thou deniest truly. In thy greatness, I am great and agree to thy will.

226 'Let us lift our voices in prayer'[14]

Let us lift our voices in prayer,
Offering up an ox to the Creator.
May this ox be permitted to grow old,
That we may gain good health.
Let us lift our voices in prayer,
Offering up an ox to the Creator.
The Creator of the sky gives us peace.
Gives us food.

227 In making a vow to God[15]

This is the goat, O my Father, continue to turn your eyes towards the sick one until he is cured. Grant my prayer, grant my prayer, O King, O earth, O heaven, let yourself be moved. If you have taken possession of him, give him back his health, O Lord, and you will receive another sacrifice.

228 If the divinity forsakes one[16]

I give to divinity Flesh my red bull;
If I am forsaken [by it], I shall give no more.
Flesh of my father, if you are clairvoyant [*tiet*]
You will spy out [*car*] the man who hates, and him who loves.

229 'Divinity: where art thou gone?'[17]

O Deng, O father, O most high Deng,
O father Deng, the great ancient one.

Dengdit refuses to hear us, Dengdit turns away.
When he is not honoured, he takes offence.
O father Deng, don't abandon me,
O father Deng, don't thrust me into the arms of the malign spirit.

I ask of Deng: Where art thou gone?
Come, father, with a gift from the man on high.
The gift is from God.
I turn to Deng, and he will listen,
I turn to him, and he will hearken.

230 Shilluk national prayer[18]

I implore thee, thou God,
I pray to thee during the night.
How are all people kept [alive] by thee all days!
And thou walkest in the midst of the high grass.
I walk with thee: when I sleep in the house, I sleep with thee.
To thee I pray for food, and thou givest it to the people;
And water to drink;
The soul is kept [alive] by thee.

There is none above thee, thou God.
Thou becamest the grandfather of Nyikang;
It is thou [Nyikang] who walkest with God,
Thou becamest the grandfather [of man], and thy son Dak.
If a famine comes, is it not given by thee?
So as this cow stands here, is it not for thee; if she dies, does her
   blood not go to thee?
Thou God, to whom shall we pray, is it not to thee?
Thou God, and thou who becamest Nyikanga and thy son Dak!
But the soul of man, is it not thine own?
It is thou who liftest us [the sick].

231 A call to pray[19]

O men and children, come along, pray to God!
O children, come along, pray to God!
Pray to our God!
Our ancestor has descended here below.
It would be madness to deride the spirits.
The spirit of the air is something great,
Pursuing us over his wide plains.

232 Left in misery[20]

I have been left in misery indeed,
God, help me!
Will you refuse [to help] the ants of this country?
When we have the clan-divinity *Deng*
Our home is called 'Lies and Confusion'.
What is all this for, O God?
Alas, I am your child.

CONFESSION AND FORGIVENESS

233 For a disobedient son[21]

O God, thou knowest this is my son; I begat him and trained him and laboured for him, and now that he should do some work for me, he refuses. In anything he does now in the world may he not prosper, until he comes back to me and begs my pardon.

234 For a repentant son[22]

O God, this is my son; he left me without any good fortune in the world because he knows I have cursed him; he has now to beg me to pull the curse as I am pulling now. Wherever he goes now may he prosper and have many children.

235 Let our shortcomings lie down[23]

LEADER: O God, be pleased to hear our prayer and let the shortcomings and failings lie down and let there be coldness.

PEOPLE: Coldness! Coldness [or Rain]!

236 Thunder, talk softly[24]

Son of Nanum!
Thou brave-loud-speaking Guru,
Talk softly please!
For I have no guilt.
Leave me alone [forgive me],
For I am become quite weak [quite stunned, perplexed].
Thou, O Guru,
Son of Nanum!

237 Forgiveness for killing the sacred animal[25]

(*a*) Someone has come to me, he has said that he killed or ate our *ntana*. Any wound that he gets is because of the *ntana* that he killed or ate. Any sickness he gets will be because of the *ntana* that he killed or ate. Let now the sickness from which he suffers be cured.

(*b*) My Father forgive me, I have killed [*name of the sacred animal*], I give you some *dege* [paste of millet flour]; I spread the *dege* in your honour. Grant me peace.
Forgive me. Grant me a happy end. Deliver me from bad sickness, deliver me from suffering.

238 A prayer of purification (or absolution)[26]

O Meketa [God], Seven Heavens, Seven Earths, Yataa [God], Earth, Fakumu, Faiyande, Heavenly children, whether or not I know how to make this sacrifice, you will trouble the one who does not know how, but the person who knows how will have not trouble. Make it blind; make it lame; carry it to the spirit in the mountain. Put it in a deep pit; place a stone upon it; let the good wind from the north and south and from the rising to the setting sun blow upon it. Let it be so, for you are able to do this. The heavenly children are offering this sacrifice, you know when I am free. You are my helper, my healer, my lifter. *Amen.*

CREDAL STATEMENTS

239 O Father, Creator, come![27]

O Father, Creator, God, I ask thy help!
I invoke thee, O my Father!
To thee, Father, I turn,
To thee, my God, I turn,
O Father, I turn to thee.
God, my Father, I pray to thee.
To thee, in time of the new moon,
I address my plea.
God recognizes my forebears who are reconciled with him.

Come all and implore God to give life to man,
Come all and receive life from God.
Rain mixed with sunbeams will gain us life.
Ask life for the flocks, the herds, and men.
Sacrifice the white ox, that God may draw nigh.
That the Father may give us life.

Deng and Abuk are invoking life.
Sacrifice the white ox, that God may draw nigh.

Now, let us reunite;
The Father has life to give,
The great Man has life.

O Father, Creator, come!
We are reunited.
Give life to herds and flocks and men.
O Father, come!
How can I reconcile myself with thee?
Go, invoke the Lord!

240 Proclaiming God's will[28]

Our Father, it is thy universe, it is thy will, let us be at peace, let the souls of the people be cool; thou art our Father, remove all evil from our path.

241 God of the Fathers[29]

Bilikonda [God] who art in the bush,
Creator Akongo [God];
Akongo of the ancestors,
Akongo of the fathers,
Our Akongo.

242 God is God[30]

Nzame [God] is on high, man is below!
Nzame is Nzame, man is man:
Each to himself, each in his dwelling.

243 God has created us[31]

O Boora Punnu [God], thou alone hast created us and hast given us the capacity to feel hunger. So we need grain and we must have fertile fields.

244 'When God created all things'[32]

In the time when God created all things, he created the sun.
And the sun is born and dies and comes again.
   He created the moon,
And the moon is born and dies and comes again.
   He created the stars,

And the stars are born and die and come again.
  He created man.
And man is born and dies and comes not again.

245 The Creator is there[33]

Truly, God the Creator is there,
And we say: Far off is Der, the Father, up there.
God, the Creator, is near,
And we say: he is not here.

246 Men refuse to listen to God who loves them[34]

On us shall descend some awful curse,
Like the curse that descended in far-off times.
Thus speaketh the Creator of men,
But the men refuse to listen.
On us shall descend some awful curse,
Like the curse that descended in far-off times:
We have but one word to say:
Idle about! Sink in sloth!
Men of such kind will gain nothing from the Father,
For they know not his voice.
He is the one who loves man.

247 'In the beginning was God'[35]

In the beginning was God,
Today is God,
Tomorrow will be God.
Who can make an image of God?
He has no body.
He is a word which comes out of your mouth.
That word! It is no more,
It is past, and still it lives!
So is God.

248 God is the source of being[36]

The source of being is above,
Which gives life to men;
For men are satisfied,
And do not die of famine,
For the Lord gives them life,
That they may live prosperously
On the earth and not die of famine.

249 'Without God we are nothing'[37]

O God of our forefathers, all our lives depend on you and without you we are nothing. It is you who look after wealth; give us plenty of good harvest, rain and wealth and children. Without you we can't live because we shall have no food or water to drink. You are the source of life. You protected us on our journey to this fertile land. Where we came from we don't know but you know. You are the God of wars and fights. Protect us against anyone who wants to harm us, especially here at my home. Here is your present.

250 A true human being[38]

I am an absolutely true Mukamba [African, human being],
Who knows that religious rites cause a baby to be born,
And knows that which is dangerous [profane],
And knows how to sacrifice in order that it may rain.
To convince you that I am a Mukamba in-and-out,
I know that a barren wife
Can give birth when rites are performed,
And know what things are harmful;
And I know that worshipping God
Makes it rain when there is a drought.

12 *Praise, joy, and thanksgiving*

Joy, praise and thanksgiving belong together, and express another dimension of African spirituality.

Prayer 251 is recorded in our sources as 'a song about God by the lizard'! Almost certainly the recorder misunderstood the word which he rendered 'lizard'. It is a prayer of praise to God for providing people with all good things which are enumerated here to include 'wives and wealth and wisdom'. Wives may represent the human dimension of good things; wealth represents the material dimension, and wisdom represents the value dimension of good things. People are called upon to beat upon their musical instruments in order to proclaim God's praise.

Prayer 252 is one of the greatest prayers in this collection. It is a prayer or song of praise to God for his greatness and great works. God piles up the rocks into mountains; he causes the waters to flow, the trees to grow, the land to be filled with mankind and the rain to fall. This is the Great Spirit, who dwells 'on high with the spirits of the great', who is gracious and merciful. For these qualities and works of God, man praises him.

The same note of appreciation of God's greatness and work is struck in prayer 253: 'Thou art the great God. . . . It is thou, thou who sittest in the highest.' This God is the creator of the heavens and the stars; he is also the 'Tower of Truth, the Bush of Truth'. God protects people and leads them. Elements of this prayer (such as the idea of God being the 'Tower of Truth' and hunting for lost souls) are probably dependent upon Christian influence since the composer of the prayer was one of the early Zulu Christians of the nineteenth century. Nevertheless the prayer as a whole is cast in traditional African style, and the specifically Christian elements appear only in the last six lines of the prayer which are given in the footnotes.

Prayer 254 opens with praise and thanksgiving to God for a deceased father. Then it addresses the departed father, enquiring why he has kept silent in the grave and why he has apparently forgotten his home. The departed father should act as an inter-

146

mediary, and pray to God for his surviving family: '. . . Why do you not pray to God? . . . You went to the presence of God, and we thought that nothing evil would befall us again after you left.' The man who is offering the prayer then turns again to God, asking him to help. But once more he asks his deceased father to join God in rescuing the family from trouble: 'Why do you not see and save us? You went to the ground, and you have forgotten that a person from another house does not guard yours.'

God is seen as the refuge in prayer 255. He is king, and must reign. He sends children to people, thus helping them build a home. The man is desperate, and pleads with God to 'be beneficent', promising to sacrifice to him a barren cow. It is reasonable to offer a cow which no longer can reproduce, since this eliminates only one animal life.

Prayer 256 opens with a line of praise to God, and seeks protection from him. It goes on to address God and Nyikang (the national founder of the Shilluk), but acknowledges God to be the giver of rain and owner of the sun. The prayer is offered in the context of sacrificing a cow which is given to both God and Nyikang. In a previous chapter we pointed out that Nyikang is a national intermediary, and he is often mentioned in Shilluk prayers because of that function.

God is acknowledged to be 'Father of the fathers' in prayer 257, and asked to give rain in order that the cattle and sheep may survive. The man who offers the prayer is hungry and thirsty. But when he has eaten and is satisfied, he will praise God in return: 'O that we may praise thee! That we may give thee in return! Thou, Father of fathers, thou, our Lord, thou O God!' Indeed the prayer is said during a dance for God.

One does not fully understand prayer 258, which in our sources is supposed to be offered 'in praise of sneezing'. It addresses someone who is not named but who is, nevertheless, in a position to give quiet sleep, and enable one to find a dead antelope in the forest.

The first ancestors of the Kikuyu are reported to have offered prayer 259 in thanksgiving to God for his glorious gifts. They were awed by God's greatness, and the man promised to follow the instructions of God. Prayer 260 is a litany shouting thanksgiving to God, possibly at a sacrificial act.

Prayers 261 and 262 indicate the joy that comes with the birth of children. The mothers are greeted with joy, and the day of birth is welcomed with joy: 'Let us all sing and praise her. . . . Greet this day with joy, Our hearts are glad.' God is acknowledged to be the creator of all human beings, and to confer great worth upon people when a child is born (262).

As we saw in chapter 9, rain is one of the most highly valued blessings in African life. People are always happy to get rain, especially when the product of their fields depends on a sufficient supply of the rain. So prayer 263 is offered in a dance of joy, celebrating the coming of the rains. Rain summons the 'people of the arrow' to take up their hoes.

In African life gratitude is expressed more in action than in words. For this reason we do not find many prayers of thanksgiving either to God or to the living dead. Instead, people sacrifice or make offerings to the spiritual realities. There is a general premise that it is the duty of the parents to look after their children, providing them with the things necessary for their lives and survival. Therefore, the children need not make verbal expressions of gratitude to their parents: instead, they do the will of their parents. So when people pose as the children of God, it is by implication held that they need not express to him their gratitude in words. It is part of his love for them to give them rain, health, protection, children, wealth, and other good things. Since God is much greater than people, they do not see clearly how they can reward him for his kindness since he owns all things and has made all things. This attitude also explains the lack of prayers of thanksgiving and praise.

PRAISE

251 Strike the chords of praise[1]

I shall sing a song of praise to God:
Strike the chords upon the drum.
God who gives us all good things—
Strike the chords upon the drum—
Wives, and wealth, and wisdom.
Strike the chords upon the drum.

252 In praise of God the Great Spirit[2]

Great Spirit!
Piler up of the rocks into towering mountains!
When thou stampest on the stone,
The dust rises and fills the land.

Hardness of the precipice;
Waters of the pool that turn
Into misty rain when stirred.
Vessel overflowing with oil!
Father of Runji,
Who seweth the heavens like cloth:
Let him knit together that which is below.
Caller forth of the branching trees:
Thou bringest forth the shoots
That they stand erect.
Thou hast filled the land with mankind,
The dust rises on high, oh Lord!
Wonderful One, thou livest
In the midst of the sheltering rocks,
Thou givest of rain to mankind:
We pray to thee,
Hear us, Lord!
Show mercy when we beseech thee, Lord.
Thou art on high with the spirits of the great.
Thou raisest the grass-covered hills
Above the earth, and createst the rivers,
Gracious One.

253 Celebrating the power of uTikxo [God][3]

Thou art the great God—he who is in heaven.
It is thou, thou Shield of Truth.
It is thou, thou Tower of Truth.
It is thou, thou Bush of Truth.
It is thou, thou, who sittest in the highest.
Thou art the Creator of life, thou madest the regions above.
The Creator who madest the heavens also.
The Maker of the stars and the Pleiades.
The shooting stars declare it unto us.
The Maker of the blind, of thine own will didst thou make them.
The Trumpet speaks—for us it calls.
Thou art the Hunter who hunts for souls.
Thou art the Leader who goes before us.
Thou art the great Mantle which covers us. . . .

(See the notes for the continuation.)

254 Praising God for one's father[4]

We praise you, you, who are God, it was you who gave me my father who begot me. I pray to you also, my father. Why did you go to earth and keep silence? Was not this your house before? When evil comes to your house, why do you not pray to God? Your house is given as a plaything to the people. You went to the presence of God, and we thought that nothing evil would befall us again after you left. Now help, God. Why do you leave this responsibility of saving on God alone? God's spirit becomes tired from work and he leaves people and they die. Why do you not see and save us? You went to the ground, and you have forgotten that a person from another house does not guard yours.

255 God as our refuge[5]

Reign! O Lord of the cattle of the Barundi,
Living Biheko,
Ryangombe of the Barundi,
Reign, our refuge.
Send me children, O Lord of the cattle of the Barundi.
Help me to build.
Grant me strength.
Be beneficent.
If I receive so much
To thee I will make a sacrifice of brew
And offer up to thee in sacrifice one barren cow.

256 'We praise thee . . .'[6]

We praise thee, thou that art God [Juok].
Protect us, we are in thy hands,
Save me.
Thou O God, and Nyikang: ye are the ones who created;
People are in your hands,
And it is thou that gavest the rain.
The sun is thine, and the river is thine.

Thou art Nyikang, thou camest from under the sun,
Thou and thy father: you two saved the earth;
And [with] thy son Dok, you subdued all the people.
The cow is here for you
And the blood will go to God and you.

257 At the sacred dance for God[7]

Thou, O Tsui-goa [God],
Thou Father of the fathers,
Thou our Father:
Let stream the thunder-cloud,
Let please live our flocks!
I am so weak indeed
From thirst,
From hunger,
O that I may eat field fruits!
Art thou, then, not our Father,
The Father of the fathers?
Thou, O Tsui-goa,
O that we may praise thee,
That we may give thee in return!
Thou, Father of fathers
Thou, our Lord
Thou, O Tsui-goa!

258 In praise of sneezing[8]

Bupsaye! Boukhwari! I pray you. I am not angry with you. Remain
with me and let me sneeze. Give me sleep and let me live so that I
can go my way, so that I can find a dead antelope in the forest and
hoist it on my shoulders, so that I can go and kill Ndlopfou bou
kene, an elephant. Now it is enough, oh, my nose.

JOY AND THANKSGIVING

259 Thanks to God for his gifts[9]

O, my Father, great Elder, I have no words to thank you, but with
your deep wisdom I am sure that you can see how much I prize your
glorious gifts. O my Father, when I look upon your greatness I am
confounded with awe. O great Elder, ruler of all things both on
heaven and on earth, I am your warrior, and I am ready to act in
accordance with your will.

260 Shouts of thanks to God[10]

LEADER: Ohee!
PEOPLE: Oheee!

LEADER: Ohee!

PEOPLE: Oheee!

ALL: Thank you: it has been cut the generation,
          This very moment as it was good the stomach of the bull.

261 Rejoicing at the birth of a child[11]

Hail the day on which this child is born.
Oh joy!
Let us all sing and praise her
That she gave birth to a son
For whom she longed.
Greet this day with joy.
Our hearts are glad.

262 Thanks for the birth of a baby[12]

O Creator, who dost all human beings create,
Thou hast a great worth on us conferred
By bringing us this little child!

263 In a joyful dance for rain[13]

An arrow for the People of the Arrow.
Swift to the figs, O Pigeons of the Rain.
Hoes for the hoers.
The flail of the thunder on the threshing-floor of God.

13 *Condemnation, blessings, and peace*

One source of great fear in African life is the formal curse. It is found and pronounced in one form or another in most African societies. It is the ultimate expression of condemnation, disapproval, punishment and dissociation. Normally the curse is pronounced over relatives, and the worst curse is one uttered by parents or aunts or uncles over children. There is also the curse on an evil-doer, made regardless of kinship ties between him and the offended party. Solemn oaths often involve an element of cursing, so that harm should befall those who are guilty or who break the oath. Prayers 264 to 268 take us into the realm of condemnation through a formal curse. In some cases the blessing and the condemnation are pronounced simultaneously (264 and 268). The practice of uttering formal curses helps to strengthen good relationships, and to control men who would cheat or steal from others. In particular, the fear of parental (or other close relational) curse seems to stablize relationships between parents and grown-up children since the latter fear to offend the former seriously lest they incur a terrible curse. Generally an older person, or one of a higher status, may curse a younger person or someone of a lower status; the offended may also pronounce a curse on the offender, especially if the latter is unknown or refuses to acknowledge his offence.

In prayer 264 someone feels lonely, as though he has been deserted. He fears that people hate him. So he pronounces a curse on those who hate him: 'A man who hates me, let him depart from me.' This means that he does not want to be with those who hate him, and does not care that they may die. At the same time, he wants to be loved, therefore he prays that: 'A man who loves me, let him come to me!' Love draws people together, hatred drives them apart.

Prayers 265 and 266 invoke destruction upon thieves. In African communities, thieves and witches are greatly hated. Indeed to this day, when discovered, thieves and witches are beaten up or even killed by the community, in many parts of Africa. Therefore the worst form of punishment is meted out to them, i.e. cursing. If the thieves are unknown the effect of the curse is dependent upon the offender being present to hear it. Even if these prayers are not directed at a named individual, it would be assumed that the thief was a member of the community and therefore he would know that the curse had been laid on him.

Prayer 267 attempts to transfer the effects of a curse and lay them upon those who have cursed another person. But this would only happen if the second person is innocent: 'But if I have myself done wrong to him, I shall die before you (the sun) go down.' The principle here is that the curse is effective only when its object is guilty.

A mixture of blessings and curses is clearly shown in 268. A severe curse is laid on 'the uncircumcised man who hates another', 'the man who does wrong', and 'the man who curses another'. 'May he perish.' There is no mercy for such people, since they destroy the community. Hatred, wrong-doing and cursing are considered in this particular society (the Meru) to be such serious evils that they invite the worst form of condemnation.

Blessings are always welcome in any community. African peoples value them and are generous in extending blessings to one another. Examples of blessings are found in prayers 269 to 283. In giving personal blessings, people commonly spit on or towards those they are blessing, or sprinkle them with water or medicinal fluids. The spittle is a symbol of acceptance, harmony, peace, and well-being; it is also a token of giving oneself to or for the person who is being blessed. The spittle unites the blesser and the blessed; it is an expression of unity between the two parties.

Prayers 269 and 270 seek blessings in terms of material welfare: goats, cattle, millet and honey (269), and the life of a young child so that he may grow to maturity. Prayer 271 blesses a son who is about to leave home, so that he may 'walk on the right path, and return in strength', to find his father still alive. At the end of this prayer (271) the father spits gently on the son and completes the blessing in the name of the clan-founder indicating that what he is doing meets the approval of the founder and family head. Other farewell formulae of blessings are found in 281.

In prayer 272 someone calls upon God, and declares that he has killed a pig, an otter and other animals, for his close departed relatives. Having done his part in remembering the living dead, he wants a blessing from God and the living dead on his long journey: 'When I go, Let there be no obstacle. . . . May I come back safely.' The man recites this prayer on three consecutive early mornings before undertaking the journey; and on the final day, he spits on the hands of his family, blesses them, and then takes leave of them. No doubt when such a prayer has been offered, he goes with a quiet mind, and they remain in peace of mind.

The blessings of prayer 273 are for material prosperity. The honey which is mentioned in this and many other Meru prayers symbolizes purity and tranquillity (sweetness) of life. Rain is the main object for blessings in number 274: 'God send us a great spreading rain that little boys may eat for themselves the herbs and salad plants . . .' Rain, as we have emphasized, is one of the most valued communal blessings in African life.

Soldiers need blessings before going to fight. We have in prayer 275 an example of one such blessing for warriors. They ask for strength to fight and that their enemies will flee from them. The prayer vividly portrays the blessings: 'May they (enemies) flee from us; Let them not see our shields.' Then the king or chief who pronounces this blessing spits on the ceremonial stone representing the invincible army which is about to go to war.

When things are not going well, the king or chief summons his people and utters a royal blessing upon them, in the words of prayer 276. He invokes God and the national or clan founder (Kunda), asking that he be given good speech, i.e. that his words of blessing his people be acceptable and effective. In fact the chief does not enumerate his blessings. He simply asks that the curse which is causing things to go wrong among his people be removed—that is the blessing that they need most. This prayer is offered early in the morning around the sacrificial tree where the people assemble for the ceremony. Prayer 277 is another royal blessing. It is rather self-centred because the king asks to 'surpass all (and). . . . To remain the conqueror'. Of course all kings and rulers of the world would pray the same for themselves!

Prayer 278 is a national blessing pronounced by the religious leader of the people. He asks God to keep the people alive, to make them bear children, and to acquire wealth. Above all he asks for blessing upon the children.

Universal blessings are requested in prayer 279: 'Let happiness come!' It asks for blessings upon people's work (water where people dig for it), upon their dwelling places, upon their religious leaders, the diviners, and upon women to bear abundantly (like the many seeds of the gourd). It also asks for blessings in protection from misfortunes and destruction on those who work against the welfare of the community. 'Hail, let happiness come!', that is the essence of all blessings.

Numbers 280 to 283 contain miscellaneous forms of short blessings. Some of these are general blessings, without indicating for what occasion they are pronounced; some are farewell blessings pronounced on the departing and those who remain behind, while others are for procreation, childbearing, fertility and longevity.

Prayers 284–288 ask for peace. Peace is perhaps the crown of African spirituality. For that reason we have put these prayers at the end of the book. People want to go through life peacefully. In prayer 284 they ask: 'O God, give us peace, give us tranquillity, and let good fortune come to us.' Their concept of peace, according to this prayer, is a state of tranquillity, a state of being free from witchcraft and ill wishes, and having enough to eat. Peace includes an abundance of rain, recovery of the sick and an ability to do one's work without trouble.

In the litany for peace (286) we are not told exactly what is the nature of peace. But true peace must come upon all: gardens, children, and the whole country. Peace for the gardens means the supply of abundant rain; peace to the children means health and normal growth; peace to the country means tranquillity, harmony among the people, and protection from disasters and national distress.

In prayer 287, peace and happiness go together. They are highlighted in the supply of meat (food), water (rain), harmony between the living and departed, and general rejoicing of the people. Therefore the people pray: 'Let Father, the God of rain, give peace.' The peace that originates from God is complete and brings happiness.

The final prayer, 288, asks for universal peace, 'May peace reign over the earth', and is a prophetic, eschatological prayer. To such a prayer, all peace-loving peoples of the world would add: AMEN, LET IT BE SO! AMEN AND AMEN.

CONDEMNATION

264 He who hates, and he who loves[1]

Come and work craftily,
Pray life from the container of seeds [the gourd].
Great Gourd [clan-divinity] of my father will help me
Even though I am left alone.

A man who hates me, let him depart from me,
A man who loves me, let him come to me,
Great Gourd of my father will help me,
Great Gourd has filled the earth.
The cow of *Deng* is milked for libations,
The cow of my father is milked,
A huge gourd of milk,
Great Gourd of my father has filled the earth.

265 'May thieves be destroyed!'[2]

O Heaven, Thou hast two eyes that see well both by day and by night. They have stolen my goods and deny it. Come and reveal them. May they be destroyed!

266 Curse to a thief[3]

You have caused me bane over my pot:
May God cause bane to you!

267 Cursing those who curse[4]

O Izuva [God], you Chief, you Murungu [God], who made men and cattle and trees and grass, you who go by overhead, take a look at him who says curse to me! When you have come up in the morning, may he see you; but when you go down in the evening, may he see you no more! But if I have myself done wrong to him, I shall die before you go down.

268 Blessing and cursing simultaneously[5]

May people be well, may they be well,
male and female, male and female,
goats and cattle,
boys and girls,
May they multiply themselves.
Let bad luck go away from us.

The [uncircumcised] man who hates another,
may he perish!
Who hates these people of mine,
may he perish!
The man who does wrong,
may he also perish!
The man who curses another, and says: 'May he perish',
He will die on the spot, cursed with the curse of the back.

BLESSINGS

269 Blessing for prosperity[6]

May you have things. Increase your goats,
cattle, millet and honey;
and if one has not them let him have.

270 For one's work to prosper[7]

Almighty God, have mercy on me.
May this child of mine see these things,
So that my work may be seen by all men,
And also those who do not trust me,
May their infidelity change!

271 A father blesses his son[8]

FATHER:	SON:
Akongo [God] of the ancestors,	mokanga
Akongo of the fathers,	mokanga
Our Akongo.	mokanga
When you go	mokanga
You must walk on the right path	mokanga
And return in strength,	mokanga
Return bearing your spear,	mokanga
Return wearing your war-belt,	mokanga
And light of foot,	mokanga.
[*spits*] Bless, Kunda, bless!	

272 Seeking blessings before a long journey[9]

Akongo [God] of my father,
Akongo of my mother,
Akongo of my mother's people,
Akongo of my sisters,
I killed a male wild-pig for you, my uncle,
I killed an otter as well;
I caught fish for you;
One day I caught twenty for you.
I killed a katukatu as well . . .
  [*blessing family*]
When I go,
Let there be no obstacle;
May I meet with nobody on the way,

May I arrive at the town where I am going;
Hard things may I avoid;
May I come back safely.
Kunda [clan father], go.

273 Invoking blessings for prosperity[10]

Get many things;
Beget many children,
Who are without blemish,
Who do not become sick,
Get honey in plenty;
Get food in plenty;
To feed your children;
And get sheep with their shepherds!

274 Blessings upon all

Heart return to the place. The seeker of the thing has found it.
Drawer, bring the little bud of the water of the rain. God send us a
great spreading rain that the little boys may eat for themselves the
herbs and salad plants of the deserted homesteads.

275 A blessing to warriors before going to fight[12]

CHIEF	WARRIORS[1]
Akongo [God] of the ancestors,	mokanga!
Akongo of the fathers,	mokanga!
Our Akongo,	mokanga!
We are going to war;	mokanga!
Give us strength	mokanga!
To fight with men;	mokanga!
Let not men see us,	mokanga!
May they flee from us;	mokanga!
Let them not see our shields;	mokanga!
Bless [*spits on the stone*], Kunda, bless!!!	

276 A royal blessing[13]

CHIEF:	PEOPLE:
Kunda,	mokanga!
I shall bless;	mokanga!
Akongo [God] of my fathers,	mokanga!
Hear me thy child,	
I pray to thee;	mokanga!

Give me good speech,	mokanga!
When I speak today;	mokanga!
No obstacle in my mouth,	mokanga!
Hear my voice in your ears;	mokanga!
Akongo of Bilikonda,	mokanga!
Akongo of the ancestors,	mokanga!
Akongo of the fathers,	mokanga!
Hear my blessing.	mokanga!
I am left in their village;	mokanga!
They gave me their village,	mokanga!
Therefore if I speak	mokanga!
You must hear my blessing.	mokanga!
I leave off.	mokanga!
Go, curse, go!	

277 Annual blessing of the country[14]

God, hear me in heaven,
The ruler of living and dead,
Enable me to increase and surpass all,
To have children and surpass the nations,
To remain the conqueror.

278 National blessing[15]

Murungu [God], we pray, help us,
That we may live, and continue to have strength;
May we bear children and cattle,
And those who have them,
They too say:
Help our children.

279 For universal blessings[16]

Hail, hail, hail! Let happiness come!
Our stools and our brooms . . .
If we dig a well, may it be at a spot where water is.
If we take water to wash our shoulders may we be refreshed.
Nyongmo give us blessing!
Mawu [God], give us blessing!
May the town be blest!
May the religious officials be blest!
May the priests be blest!
May the mouthpieces of the divinities be blest!

May we be filled going and coming.
May we not drop our head-pads except at the big pot.
May our fruitful women be like gourds
And may they bring forth and sit down.
May misfortunes jump over us.
If today anyone takes up a stick or a stone against this our blessing,
   do we bless him?
May Wednesday and Sunday kill him.
May we flog him.
Hail, let happiness come!
Is our voice one?
Hail, let happiness come!

280 General blessings[17]

(*a*) May the God of Banyarwanda bless you!
(*b*) May God make your forehead big!
(*c*) May God give you a clean face [i.e. good fortune]!
(*d*) May God be good to you!
(*e*) May God guard you!
(*f*) May God protect you!
(*g*) May God make your feet light!

281 Farewell blessings[18]

(*a*) May God go with you!
(*b*) Go nicely: may your path be swept [of danger].
   God go with you, and may you be left [escape from] the mishaps
   ahead!
(*c*) May you go with God!
(*d*) Let God bear you in peace like a young shoot!
(*e*) May you meet with the Kindly-disposed One!
(*f*) May God take care of you!
(*g*) May God walk you well!
(*h*) May you pass the night with God!
(*i*) May you remain with God!
(*j*) May God be with you who remain behind!
(*k*) May you stay with God!

282 Procreation blessings[19]

(*a*) You want fruit: may God give you fruit!
(*b*) May God give you many children!

283 Longevity blessings[20]

(*a*) May God give you long life!

(*b*) May God preserve and keep you until you see your children's children!

PEACE

284 Invocations for peace, rain and health[21]

O God, give us peace, give us tranquillity, and let good fortune come to us.

Let the one who put a jinx on the village die. Let him die, he who thought evil thoughts against us. Also give us fish.

O God, give us rain, we are in misery, we suffer with our sons. Send us the clouds that bring the rain. We pray Thee, O Lord our Father, to send us the rain.

Let her who is sick, O God, receive from thee health and peace, and her village and her children and her husband. Let her get up and go to work, let her work in the kitchen, let her find peace again.

285 'Peace be with us'[22]

LEADER: Say ye, the elders may have wisdom and speak with one voice.

GROUP: Praise ye Ngai [God]. Peace be with us.

LEADER: Say ye that the country may have tranquillity and the people may continue to increase.

GROUP: Praise ye Ngai. Peace be with us.

LEADER: Say ye that the people and the flocks and herds may prosper and be free from illness.

286 A litany of peace[23]

LEADER:	OTHER PEOPLE:
Say peace!	O peace!
Peace to children!	O peace to children!
Peace to the country!	O peace to the country!
Peace to the gardens!	O peace to the gardens!

287 Peace and happiness[24]

Exalted! Exalted! Exalted!
Ho, priestly people!

Let Bleku [rain] give peace.
Meat, meat,
Water, water,
Let blessings bless:
Masses of food!

Hail, hail, hail!
Let happiness come!
Are our voices one?
Let Grandfather Sakumo give peace.
Let Akpitioko give peace.
Let Otshiama give peace.
Let Awudu, the Almighty, give peace.
Let Father, the God of rain, give peace.
Hail, hail, hail!
Let happiness come!

288 For universal peace[25]

May peace reign over the earth, may the gourd cup agree with the
vessel. May their heads agree and every ill word be driven out into
the wilderness, into the virgin forest.

Notes

CHAPTER 2

1. Pygmies, Zaire; di Nola, p. 7. The prayer is chanted by women, walking. The sources do not indicate which Pygmies have this prayer.

2. Banyankore, Uganda; Bamunoba. This prayer is made by the woman head of the family, to God, squeezing leaves of *omuhiire* (*physalia minima*) and sprinkling their juice over the fire in the house.

3. Vugusu, Kenya; Mbiti, p. 61. Spitting is a symbol of blessing, and accompanies the utterance of good wishes, fortune or blessings in many African societies.

4. Abaluyia, Kenya; Mbiti, p. 195. This prayer is commonly used by old men The sun is a symbol of God's perpetual presence.

5. Nandi, Kenya; Hollis, II, p. 42. This invocation is preceded by a short ritual of spitting towards the sun, in the morning.

6. Konde, Tanzania; di Nola, p. 34.

7. Maasai, Kenya; di Nola, p. 37.

8. Nandi, Kenya; Hollis, II, p. 43. This invocation is made by an elder who accompanies a cattle raiding party. In making it he faces the rising sun, spits and invokes God for success in their undertaking.

9. Giur, Sudan?; di Nola, pp. 28f.

10. Dinka, Sudan; di Nola, p. 23.

11. Galla, Ethiopia and Kenya; Mbiti, p. 197.

12. Nandi, Kenya; Hollis, II, p. 42. This prayer is said by all adults, twice a day. (The version is a 'free translation' in the original source.)

13. Galla, Ethiopia and Kenya; di Nola, p. 40.

14. Nandi, Kenya; Hollis, II, pp. 42 f.

15. Mensa, Ethiopia; di Nola, p. 41. This is a prayer at the new moon.

16. 'Bushmen', South Africa; Shorter, p. 4. It is not specified which group of people is meant here by 'Bushmen', a term which is not very fitting today.

17. Ashanti, Ghana; Rattray, pp. 128, 130, 134, 137. The Odwira ceremony (or The Yam Custom) is presided over or conducted by the Ashanti king (at least formerly).

18. Nama, South Africa: Smith, p. 96. The 'yearly killing' (*guri-ab*) is the most important festival of the Nama people. It is held when the rains are due. All the people assemble at the chief's summons, each family contributing milk or a pregnant ewe or cow which is sacrificed. They dance, sing and call upon God to send plentiful rains. This is one such prayer hymn.

19. Ga, Ghana; Field, I, p. 51. This an annual festival of the Ga people, marking the end of one agricultural year and the beginning of another, at harvest time. Houses are purified, people eat, drink and rejoice, and invite their

living dead to join them and renew their protection over the living. At this occasion of rejoicing, they greet and bless one another with the words of this prayer.

CHAPTER 3

1. Fang, Cameroon and Gabon; di Nola, p. 10.
2. Ashanti, Ghana; Rattray, p. 139. This prayer is (was) offered at the end of a national day of purification when sheep are sacrificed to the spirits of departed kings, and wine and yams offered to them.
3. Mende, Sierra Leone; Butt-Thompson, p. 202. This prayer is offered by the leader of the Poro society, at the opening of an annual festival.
4. Yoruba, Nigeria; Idowu, p. 74. The word 'Death' refers to any person in high position who has power over life and death of other people. The prayer is not addressed to death as such!
5. Anuak, Sudan; Mbiti, p. 195.
6. Luguru, Tanzania; Shorter, p. 23.
7. Cameroon; di Nola, p. 39.
8. Dinka, Sudan; di Nola, p. 24.
9. Ngombe, Zaire; J. Davidson in Smith, p. 175. Kunda is the founder or father of many clans among the Ngombe.
10. Meru, Kenya; Bernardi, p. 129. The prayer is made by the medicine-man when treating a sick person.
11. Banyankore, Uganda; Bamunoba, personal communication. An officiant offers this prayer after lighting a fire and ritually killing a goat at the shrine of a major or tribal spirit (*emandwa*).
12. Banyankore, Uganda; Bamunoba, ibid. The prayer is made at a symbolic initiation to a spirit (*emandwa*) cult: later the patient is in reality initiated, when he has recovered.
13. Chewa, Malawi; T. C. Young in Smith, p. 44. This prayer is made by the headman who summons people at dawn and, calling on the departed fore-fathers, he spurts gruel on the ground and publicly asks for their aid.
14. Dinka, Sudan; Lienhardt, pp. 221 f. Akol is the name of the sick man: Macardit ('the great black one') is one of the 'free-divinities' and is thought to kill people.
15. Langi, Uganda; Hayley, p. 144.
16. Langi, Uganda; Driberg, I, pp. 240 f.
17. Langi, Uganda; Hayley, pp. 117 f.
18. Ngoni, Malawi; Read, pp. 198 f. The second plea is made when the spirits have 'refused' to heal the sick.
19. Pondo, South Africa; Hunter, p. 247.
20. Pondo, South Africa; Hunter, ibid.
21. Aro, Sierra Leone; Butt-Thompson, p. 202.
22. Kafu-Bullom, Sierra Leone; Butt-Thompson, ibid.
23. Dinka, Sudan; Lienhardt, pp. 222 ff. The prayer is led by 'a master of the fishing-spear of the Pagong clan'.

CHAPTER 4

1. Nandi, Kenya; Hollis, II, p. 44.
2. Nandi, Kenya; Hollis, ibid.
3. Nandi, Kenya; Hollis, II, p. 45.
4. Nandi, Kenya; Hollis, II, p. 46.
5. Nandi, Kenya; Hollis, ibid.
6. Nuba, Sudan; Mbiti, p. 60. The first of these two invocations is made at the beginning of the rain season, at a ceremony for the increase of cattle.
7. Kikuyu, Kenya; Mbiti, p. 198. This invocation is made by the head of the family.
8. Meru, Kenya; Bernardi, p. 113. The Mugwe is a traditional religious leader of the Meru, and it is he who leads the people in invoking God for the increase of cattle and children.
9. Didinga, Sudan; Driberg, II, pp. 83 f. At the time of recording, this prayer was led by one, Lokumamoi, while his followers, kneeling and posed with their weapons as for defence, joined in the responses; but it is not indicated which are the responses.
10. Maasai, Kenya and Tanzania; Hollis, I, p. 350. This prayer is sung by the warriors after a successful raid when they have slaughtered their enemy and are driving off the cattle. Lenana was a famous ritual expert (*Laibon*) who succeeded his father on the latter's death in 1890 and was a leading figure in the so-called Masai Agreements with the British in 1904 and 1911 respectively, by which a good deal of Maasai land was handed over to British settlers.
11. Namaqua, Namibia (South West Africa); De Quatrefages, p. 213.
12. Meru, Kenya; Bernardi, p. 115. The prayer was offered by the Mugwe (religious leader) of the Imenti area.
13. Zulu, South Africa; di Nola, p. 227.
14. Dinka, Sudan; Lienhardt, p. 44. The use of 'husband' to refer to God is obviously metaphorical since it is he who causes both women and cows to bear.
15. Nandi, Kenya; Mbiti, p. 60. This is a ceremonial prayer.
16. Pygmy, Zaire; di Nola, p. 7. Our sources do not indicate from which Pygmy people this prayer is taken. It is addressed to 'the serpent Totemico, or Celeste' held to be a totem of 'the tribe's guardian'. The snake is probably a python.

CHAPTER 5

1. Lozi, Zambia; di Nola, p. 38.
2. Dogon, Upper Volta and Mali; Griaule, pp. 138 f. This prayer is recited at a national sacrificial ceremony marking the time of sowing.
3. Didinga, Sudan; Driberg, II, pp. 142 f.
4. Didinga, Sudan; Driberg, II, p. 148. An animal is sacrificed and its blood sprinkled over the ground when this prayer is recited.

5. Kikuyu, Kenya; di Nola, p. 37. Both Ngai and Mwene-Nyaga are names of God.

6. Banyankore, Uganda; Bamunoba, personal communication. When millet is ready for eating, a millet dish is prepared and offered at the family shrines by the husband and wife, to God and the spirits, before any human being has eaten of the new crop. This offering is a form of dedicating and sanctifying the whole crop, and thus making it 'safe' for human consumption.

7. Konde, Tanzania; di Nola, p. 35.

8. Nandi, Kenya; Hollis, II, p. 47. The prayer is recited by the head of the family at harvest time, and other people repeat the words after him.

9. Nandi, Kenya; Hollis, ibid.

10. Banyankore, Uganda; Bamunoba, ibid. This prayer, like number 71 (note 6 *supra*), is recited when the family makes a millet meal with the first grains to be harvested, and the husband takes portions of it together with beer, to the family shrine. These are offered to the spirit (Omuzimu) of his deceased father, which he addresses in a plurality. Before the spirit symbolically eats of the new harvest, nobody is allowed to eat of the first fruit of the fields.

11. Ashanti, Ghana; Rattray, pp. 45 f. This prayer is taught to a novice when he enters his third and final year of training as a priest and diviner. He is taught water-gazing, divining, impregnating charms with spirits, listening to and interpreting voices of the trees, and so on. The prayer indicates some of the concerns he has to face.

12. Fang, Cameroon and Gabon; di Nola, p. 9.

13. Giur, Sudan?; di Nola, p. 30. The medicine-man who chants this prayer shakes a weapon over the patient, and sprinkles blood (from a sacrificed sheep) and water over all those who are present. This sprinkling is a symbol of purification from disease and misfortunes.

14. Ewe, Dahomey, Ghana and Togo; di Nola, p. 41.

15. Pondo, South Africa; Hunter, p. 248.

16. Pondo, South Africa; Hunter, p. 242.

17. Zande, Sudan; Evans-Pritchard, I, p. 344, for both this and the following invocation. An elder recites the oracle.

18. Nandi, Kenya; Hollis, II, p. 37. This formula is recited by smiths when searching for iron ore.

19. Zande, Sudan; Evans-Pritchard, I, p. 340.

20. Ngombe, Zaire, J. Davidson in Smith, pp. 171 f. At the hunting grounds a special tree is cut, planted on the ground and its leaves tied to the base. It is known as *edatito* which means 'there will be animals'. The leader of the hunting group chants this invocation, while the rest join at the end with a word of agreement, *mokanga*.

21. Ila, Zambia; Mbiti, p. 199. When the hunters have no success, they sit down in a circle, and the oldest man among them goes to the centre and leads the rest in this prayer. When they succeed in their hunting, they cut pieces of meat and offer them to God in an act of thanksgiving, using the formula (c).

22. Tanzania (people unspecified); di Nola, p. 40.
23. Lobi, Ivory Coast; di Nola, p. 32. The fisherman offers a baby chick for divination purposes, along the river at a point frequented by crocodiles and hippopotamuses, and recites this prayer.
24. Zande, Sudan; Evans-Pritchard, I, p. 469.
25. Central or southern Africa; di Nola, p. 12. This prayer is offered by a medicine-man in the doorway of someone who is about to go on a journey. He spits a medicinal preparation on the traveller and wipes his body with it.

CHAPTER 6

1. Ewe, Ghana, Dahomey and Togo; di Nola, p. 42.
2. Konde, Tanzania; di Nola, p. 35.
3. Chagga, Tanzania; di Nola, p. 40.
4. Giur, Sudan?; di Nola, p. 29 f.
5. Didinga, Sudan; Driberg, p. 38 f.
6. Didinga, Sudan; Driberg, p. 44.
7. Maasai, Kenya and Tanzania; di Nola, p. 36 f.
8. Nandi, Kenya; Hollis, II, p. 45.
9. Nandi, Kenya; Hollis, II, p. 45.
10. Maasai, Kenya and Tanzania; Hollis, I, p. 351.
11. Meru, Kenya; Bernardi, p. 113.
12. Maasai, Kenya and Tanzania; Hollis, I, p. 351. This is chanted by the whole assembly of people gathered together.
13. Banyankore, Uganda; Bamunoba, personal communication.
14. Meru, Kenya; Mbiti, p. 202.
15. Nuer, Sudan; Evans-Pritchard, II, p. 46 f. When the warriors go to war, the war diviner runs along their flanks encouraging them and waving a spear decorated with ostrich plumes. This recitation is addressed in form of a hymn to *mani* (spirit of the air) and *dayim* ('son of God', about which I am unable to find more information).
16. Yoruba, Nigeria; Idowu, p. 27.
17. Dinka, Sudan; Lienhardt, p. 228. Another paragraph follows this part of the prayer, warning the man who has bewitched the other that he will soon get his reward.
18. Bakuba, Zaire; J. Vansina in Douglas and Kaberry, p. 249. These words are addressed to a poison-bearing tree in the forest, by a diviner.
19. Malagasy, Madagascar; di Nola, p. 17. It is said that both 'Zanar and Niang are the creators of the world'.
20. Kham (Bushmen), South Africa; Smith, p. 90.
21. Barolong, South Africa; Smith, p. 121. This prayer was first recorded in 1843.
22. Konde, Tanzania; di Nola, p. 35.

23. Lobi, Ivory Coast; di Nola, p. 32. This prayer is chanted by the priest over the new territory when the people are forced by famine to move to a new settlement.

24. Dinka, Sudan; Seligman, p. 180. This prayer hymn is sung during a time of sickness, drought or other natural disaster.

25. Dinka, Sudan; Lienhardt, p. 94. Deng is one of the divinities (*yeeth*) which have relationships with individuals and families. Lienhardt calls them 'free-divinities' (p. 30).

26. Dinka, Sudan; di Nola, p. 22.

27. Barundi and Banyarwanda, Burundi and Rwanda; R. Guillebaud in Smith, pp. 192 f.

28. Barundi, Burundi; R. Guillebaud in Smith, p. 198. This lament normally ends in tears. It may also be used by a woman who has been driven away by her husband.

29. Banyarwanda, Ruanda; R. Guillebaud, op. cit., pp. 198 f.

30. Abaluyia, Kenya; H. Merritt, in a draft of a doctorate thesis for the University of Nairobi, Kenya, 1974.

31. Malagasy, Madagascar; di Nola, p. 18.

32. Dinka, Sudan; Lienhardt, p. 228.

CHAPTER 7

1. Giur, Sudan?; di Nola, pp. 30 f.

2. Ewe, Ghana, Dahomey and Togo; di Nola, p. 42.

3. Mende, Sierra Leone; Butt-Thompson, pp. 201 f.

4. Akim-Kotoku, Ghana; Field, II, p. 136.

5. Dinka, Sudan; Seligman, p. 166. The prayer is recited after the birth of twins.

6. Lango, Uganda; di Nola, p. 33. The prayer is offered during a purification ceremony (*gayo tango*) at the birth of twins. All men are smeared with flour. The officiating old woman spits on a millet stalk, brandishes it around, and rubs soup from a pot on the breasts of men and women while reciting this prayer.

7. Nandi, Kenya; Hollis, II, p. 65. This ceremony is performed when the infant is about four months old. It is washed in the undigested food from the stomach of an animal which has been killed for the occasion.

8. Ashanti, Ghana; Rattray, p. 64. At the naming ceremony the mother places the infant on the knees of one of its grandparents after it has been bathed and given a new cloth by its father. A boy would normally be named after a grandfather, and a girl after a female relative on the paternal side. The grandparent recites the words of this prayer during the ceremony.

9. Karimojong, Uganda; Hudson, pp. 165ff. At this initiation ceremony it is the elders of a senior generation set who induct the new group. Each initiate is smeared with chyme on nearly his whole body and blessed: 'Be well. Grow old. Become wealthy in stock. Become an elder!' This takes

place inside an enclosure. Round the enclosure or outside, a prayer leader recites the prayer litany given here, and all the people assembled for the big occasion respond accordingly. The initiating age or generation set is known as the Mountains, and the new group is Gazelles; Ngipian is the territorial section.

10. Fang, Cameroon and Gabon; di Nola, p. 7. The skulls of tribal forefathers are kept in a coffer. This prayer is recited by the head of the family during the initiation ceremony for the young at which the coffer is held up for the occasion.

11. Abaluyia (Bukusu), Kenya; H. Merritt, in a draft of a doctorate thesis for the University of Nairobi, Kenya, 1974. The prayer is offered in the morning near the home compound of the circumcision candidate, by his grandfather who also places a basket over the white cock until 4 p.m. when it is released unceremoniously.

12. Ashanti, Ghana; Rattray, pp. 70, 72. When a girl first menstruates, she informs her mother who then takes wine and pours a little of it as libation on the ground saying the first of these prayers. Another invocation is number 136. For this, the girl is taken round the waist by a woman whose first-born child is still alive. Between the girl's legs is tucked a loin cloth. Later this cloth and a sponge with which she is bathed, as well as an egg, are placed in the stream at which the words of this invocation are recited.

13. Banyarwanda, Rwanda; di Nola, p. 41.

14. Ashanti, Ghana; Rattray, p. 160. When a child who is less than eight days old dies, the maternal grandmother takes mashed yams or plantain (*eto*) and eggs and goes with the child's mother to the cross-roads where she recites this prayer.

15. Nuba, Sudan; Mbiti, p. 92. The southern Nuba from whom this prayer comes are matrilineal, hence their image of God as female to whom they refer as 'the Great Mother'.

16. Dinka, Sudan; Di Nola, p. 23.

17. Pygmies (unspecified), Zaire; di Nola, pp. 4. f.

18. Ovambo, Namibia (S.W. Africa); Smith, p. 148.

19. —?—, Zaire; di Nola, p. 40.

20. —?—, South Africa; di Nola, p. 11.

21. Ashanti, Ghana; Busia, p. 42.

22. Hottentot, South Africa; Shorter, p. 16.

23. Bambara, Mali; di Nola, p. 16. These four invocations come from a set of complicated funeral rites. Invocation (a) is recited by the officiant (priest or medicine-man) at the beginning of the ceremony; (b) closes the first part of the ceremony; (c) is recited when the officiant of the rites leans over the grave and pours water from a gourd onto the body; and (d) is recited by women clapping their hands while the earth is shovelled into the grave.

24. Basoga, Uganda; Mbotana, p. 1. This wailing prayer is uttered by the widow of a dead man, shortly after death. Other relatives join in similar words.

25. Nuer, Sudan; Evans-Pritchard, II, 45 f. '*Deng* is the greatest of the spirits of the air'; *buk* is another spirit of the air; *pake* (from Arabic *faki* which means a fakir or holy man) is used by the Nuer to refer to an Arab pedlar or merchant.

CHAPTER 8

1. Acholi, Uganda; Russell, pp. 15 f.
2. Maragoli, Kenya; Wagner, p. 107.
3. Kafu-Bullom, Sierra Leone; Butt-Thompson, pp. 199 ff.
4. —?—, East or Central Africa; di Nola, pp. 12 f.
5. Bambara, Mali; di Nola, p. 15.
6. Zulu, South Africa; di Nola, p. 31.
7. Chagga, Tanzania; di Nola, p. 40.
8. Banyankore, Uganda; Bamunoba, personal communication.
9. Kaonde, Zambia; Melland, p. 148.
10. Baluba, Zaire; Campbell, p. 80.
11. Fon, Dahomey; Herskovits, p. 237.
12. Ngoni, Malawi; di Nola, p. 14.
13. Ashanti, Ghana; Rattray, pp. 6 f. The two prayers are addressed to the spirits of the tree and the elephant, respectively. The tree and the ear of the elephant are used for making the talking drum (*ntumpane*).
14. Ashanti, Ghana; Rattray, p. 278.

CHAPTER 9

1. Langi, Uganda; Driberg, I, pp. 250 f.
2. Giur, Sudan?; di Nola, p. 29. This prayer is recited at a public ceremony, and is conducted by a person who is possessed by 'the creative spirit'.
3. —?—, East or Central Africa; di Nola, p. 13.
4. Ila, Zambia; Smith and Dale, p. 209.
5. Suk, Kenya; Beech, p. 16.
6. Dinka, Sudan; di Nola, p. 22.
7. Nandi, Kenya; Hollis, II, p. 48.
8. Dinka, Sudan; di Nola, p. 25.
9. Maasai, Kenya and Tanzania; Hollis, I, p. 347. The women collect themselves together, tie bundles of grass on their clothes and sing this prayer. Mbatian was a great ritual expert (*Laibon*) who died in 1890; Nasira was one of his daughters.
10. Maasai, Kenya and Tanzania; Hollis, I, p. 348. When there is a drought, old men make a bonfire into which a medicine-man throws a 'medicine' called *ol-okora*. They encircle the fire and sing this prayer for rain.
11. Hottentots, South Africa; di Nola, p. 34.
12. Koranna, South Africa; Smith, p. 95. When the time of need arises, people kill an animal, burn its bones and fat, and as the scent ascends to the sky, they offer this prayer.

13. Bakango, Zaire; di Nola, p. 35.
14. Pygmies, Zaire; di Nola, p. 7.
15. Tiv, Nigeria; East, p. 233.

CHAPTER 10

1. Dinka, Sudan; Lienhardt, p. 103. Deng is one of the 'free-divinities', Garang and Abuk were "the first human beings . . . living on earth'. (Here and in other prayers they are among the 'free-divinities'.) To 'go through your legs' is a reference to a ritual in which the sick person crawls through the legs of a medicine-man, leaving behind the sickness.

2. —?—, South Africa; di Nola, p. II. This prayer is offered at the rites performed in order to give legitimacy to marriages between individuals who are otherwise forbidden to enter into matrimony. At these rites, the couple concerned eat the liver of a sacrificed animal, thereby removing the taboo against their marriage. The second part of the prayer is offered by the bride's father while two goats are sacrificed in front of her mother's house.

3. Tswana (Bechuana), Botswana; Brown, p. 157. This formula is uttered when a couple is being purified before they can live together as husband and wife; and their house is purified as well.

4. Banyankore, Uganda; Bamunoba, private communication. An officiant dips a bundle (*omuhambo*) of special white herbs into a pot of beer. Then he waves the bundle in all directions of the compass, and recites this prayer. This rite is performed before making an offering to general spirits (*emandwa*).

5. Didinga, Sudan; Driberg, II, pp. 160 f.

6. Bakuba, Zaire; J. Vansina in Douglas and Kaberry, p. 250.

7. Bambuti, Zaire; Mbiti, p. 196. When thunderstorms arise and the people become frightened, they burn incense and call upon God, using this invocation.

8. Zulu, South Africa; di Nola, p. 31.

9. Bambara, Mali; di Nola, pp. 15 f. There exists a secret society or association, *n'tomo*, into which a would-be member has to be initiated. For this, he offers a chicken to the leader, prostrates himself before the initiation tree, and swears that he will never reveal the rites and teachings of the society to those who are not initiated. The society holds a great annual festival at which members make a sacrifice in honour of their brotherhood. This prayer accompanies the sacrifice which ends this festival.

10. Acholi, Uganda; Russell, p. 14.

11. Banyankore, Uganda; Bamunoba, personal communication. If the goat given to the family spirit (*omuzimu*) grows old or has to be killed, the head of the family exchanges it for a new one. It is on such occasion that this invocation is offered, to ensure that the exchange is acceptable to the spirit.

12. Banyankore, Uganda; Bamunoba, personal communication. A cow put aside for the ancestral ghost is known as *enzimu* (spirit's cow). All its calves belong to the spirit; and their milk is drunk only by unmarried boys and

girls. At the appearance of the new moon, milk from the *enzimu* is put aside in a pot by the chief woman in the home who offers it to the living dead. The pot is covered and left at the spirit's shrine.

13. Banyankore, Uganda; Bamunoba, personal communication. This invocation is said by the chief sacrificer while he throws pieces of meat into the air, offering the sacrificial animal (cow) first to God. The remaining meat is eaten within the enclosure of the shrine of the clan spirits, in this case the Bahinda clan.

14. Chagga, Tanzania; Mbiti, p. 198. The people face Mount Kilimanjaro, at whose foot they live, while reciting this sacrificial prayer.

15. Adhola, Uganda; J. S. Owor, '*Lamirok gi Chowirok* (Religious Beliefs and Practices)', Occasional Research paper No. 58, Department of Religious Studies and Philosophy, Makerere University, Kampala, 1972, p. 4.

16. Kikuyu, Kenya; Routledge, p. 231. The prayer was offered by a leading Kikuyu, Munge, while the people stood. Afterwards a sheep was slaughtered. The occasion was called for by the arrival of two visitors, the Routledges, from Britain in 1908.

17. Ashanti, Ghana; Rattray, p. 47. This invocation is made after the ceremony of inaugurating (ordaining) a new priest who has completed three years of training. Drummers and singers assemble round a fire, and the new priest is dressed up in priestly clothes and ornaments. His hair is cut and put into a pot. The older priest examines his head and removes any bad things 'which cause a priest to do wrong', and puts them into the pot together with the hair. The new priest dances all night. Early the next morning the pot is placed on the head of a young boy who has to run off with it and place it on the ground upside-down, away from the compound. The new priest 'cuts' a sheep for his new divinity, indicating that he has now been united with it.

18. Pygmies, Zaire; di Nola, p. 4. The infant is lifted towards the sun while the father says this prayer.

19. —?—, South Africa; di Nola, p. 10. The prayer is a formula for a ceremony called *Kou Biyeketa*.

20. Dogon, Mali and Upper Volta; Griaule, p. 164.

21. Dinka, Sudan; Seligman, pp. 189 f. Daiyim is one of the divinities; Garang and Abuk were the first human beings living on the earth, according to Dinka mythology.

22. Yoruba, Nigeria; Idowu, p. 114. This is sung in praise of Orisa-nla, the divinity thought to be God's deputy on earth in creative and executive functions. This and other songs are an expression of rejoicing that offerings have been accepted.

23. Nyole (Abaluyia), Kenya; Wagner, p. 3. The prayer is said before building a new house. This and the next prayer, 205, belong together.

24. Nyole (Abaluyia), Kenya; Wagner, p. 4. The prayer is said before thatching the roof of a newly built house. This and the previous prayer, 204, belong together.

25. Dogon, Mali and Upper Volta; Griaule, p. 94.

26. Ashanti, Ghana; Rattray, p. 138. At the time when this prayer was recorded, the king performed the ceremony of sprinkling the Golden Stool. He held a branch of a plant *bosommuru adwira*, which he dipped into a large brass basin filled with water. Then he sprinkled the Golden Stool, reciting the words of this prayer.

27. —?—, South Africa; di Nola, p. 13. The maker of the new sword rubs it with a piece of 'medicinal' wood, *kianduri*, while reciting the words of this prayer.

28. Giur, Sudan?; di Nola, p. 28. It is not known for certain how this 'Magic Spear' originated. When the Giur go to war, the sword is carried in front of their ranks, and this prayer is recited by the sword bearer.

29. Banyankore; Uganda; P. Kasenene, 'Beliefs, Rituals and Taboos surrounding Beer-trough Making among the Banyankore', Occasional Research Paper No. 122, Department of Religious Studies and Philosophy, Makerere University, Kampala, 1973, p. 5. The person who makes a beer-trough prays over it, having tied a shrub round it, or round the tree out of which it would be made if he has not already made it. Kazooba, Rugaba and Nyamu-hanga are names of God, describing various attributes of him.

30. Banyoro, Uganda; Roscoe, p. 183.

31. Akim-Kotoku, Ghana; Field, II, p. 166.

CHAPTER 11

1. Galla, Kenya and Ethiopia; Shorter, p. 14.

2. Shilluk, Sudan; di Nola, p. 26.

3. Shilluk, Sudan; di Nola, p. 27.

4. Dinka, Sudan; Lienhardt, p. 218. In one of the Dinka myths it is said that Aiwel Longar 'was the first to be created. . . . "He had just come from the hand of God, he was at the head (source) of life". ' Jiel was 'the husband of the mother of the first master of the fishing-spear'. Pagong is the clan of Longar.

5. Chagga, Tanzania; di Nola, p. 39. This invocation is recited every morning when one has made a ritual spitting towards the sun.

6. Dinka, Sudan; Lienhardt, p. 282. To 'hold a feast against' someone means to make war, to attack.

7. Dinka, Sudan; Lienhardt, p. 188. It is recounted that Aiwel Longar (note 4 *supra*) came out of the river Nile and sat on the bank at a place called Gutacol. He then sang this song. Flesh is a divinity of Aiwel, said to have been 'brought by the wind from behind'.

8. Dinka, Sudan; di Nola, p. 23.

9. Dinka, Sudan; di Nola, p. 24.

10. Maasai, Kenya and Tanzania; Hollis, I, p. 346.

11. Shilluk, Sudan; di Nola, p. 26.

12. Giur, Sudan?; di Nola, p. 28.

13. Ewe, Dahomey, Ghana and Togo; di Nola, p. 42.

14. Dinka, Sudan; di Nola, p. 25.

15. Chagga, Tanzania; di Nola, p. 39.
16. Dinka, Sudan; Lienhardt, p. 142.
17. Dinka, Sudan; di Nola, p. 24. Deng and Dengdit are names of divinities.
18. Shilluk, Sudan; Mbiti, p. 204.
19. Langi, Uganda; di Nola, p. 33.
20. Dinka, Sudan; Lienhardt, p. 45.
21. Mende, Sierra Leone: Mbiti, p. 201. When the son repents and returns home, after facing the miseries mentioned in this prayer, his father prays to have him reaccepted in the family according to the next prayer 234.
22. Mende, Sierra Leone; Mbiti, ibid. This prayer has meaning in the light of the previous one, 233. It removes the curse on the now repentant son, which his father had invoked in the preceding prayer.
23. Tswana, Botswana; Brown, p. 156. The priest smears the body of the person who had done wrong, with a medicinal mixture, and utters the words of this prayer of absolution.
24. Namaqua, South Africa; Quatrefages, p. 219. This is a prayer hymn.
25. Bambara, Mali; di Nola, p. 15. If one offends the community by killing or otherwise injuring the sacred animal, *n'tana*, confession is made to an older member of the group. The older member performs a short ritual of bending a fistful of straw into two, and puts flowers where the straw bends. The guilty man crouches at his feet, and the officiant waves the straw and flowers over his head, making a circle, three times, while saying the first of these two prayers absolving the guilty man. The offender then recites the second prayer, for forgiveness.
26. Kono, Sierra Leone; R. T. Parsons in Smith, p. 268. The ancient word for God in the Kono language is Meketa; but Tataa is now more commonly used. This prayer is offered by the priest, *bengene*, who is a pure man with *kasimanyina* ('a spirit against which there is no accusation'). The occasion for this prayer arises when crops fail or disease breaks, or other misfortunes hit the people. They then assemble, bringing gifts of cotton, rice, chickens and so on. The bengene calls out various misdeeds that may have brought about the defilement of the land, and urges the people to acknowledge their misdoings. He then blesses them, sprinkling water on them. If there is a breach against sexual morality, then this prayer is said, after the guilty persons are taken to him and, in the presence of the villagers, loudly confess their misdoings. Then, on their behalf, the priest offers this prayer, relaying it through the deceased bengene. A fowl is scarificed, its blood dripped on two stones (representing male and female); and the priest sprinkles 'medicine' on the forest to make it clean and able again to yield crops. The 'Amina' at the end might be a later addition to the formula, through contact with Christian praying.
27. Dinka, Sudan; di Nola, pp. 21 f.
28. Nuer, Sudan; Mbiti, p. 203.
29. Ngombe, Zaire; J. Davidson in Smith, p. 166. Bilikonda is a praise name for God, and means: 'the unendingness of the forest', that is, the everlasting one, the Eternal.

30. Fang, Cameroon and Gabon; di Nola, p. 8.

31. Konde, Tanzania; di Nola, p. 35.

32. Dinka, Sudan; di Nola, p. 20.

33. Dinka, Sudan; di Nola, p. 21.

34. Dinka, Sudan; di Nola, p. 21.

35. Pygmies, Zaire; Mbiti, p. 23.

36. Zulu, South Africa; Mbiti, p. 60.

37. Adhola, Uganda; P. Owere, 'Bura the Adhola God, before and after the Coming of the Catholic Church to Padhola', Occasional Research Paper No. 168, Department of Religious Studies and Philosophy, Makerere University, Kampala, 1973, p. 5. The prayer is offered at a time of sacrificing.

38. Akamba, Kenya; Ndeti, pp. 93 f., my own translation.

CHAPTER 12

1. Baluba, Zaire; Campbell, p. 247.

2. Shona, Zimbabwe (Rhodesia); Smith, p. 127.

3. Zulu, South Africa; Smith, p. 102. The prayer was composed by Unsikana, a Zulu Christian, in the early nineteenth century. The concluding six lines of the prayer have clearly Christian concepts and are as follows:
    Thou art He whose hands are with wounds.
    Thou art He whose feet are with wounds.
    Thou art He whose blood is a trickling stream—and why?
    Thou art He whose blood was spilled for us.
    For this great price we call,
    For thine own place we call.

4. Shilluk, Sudan; di Nola, p. 26.

5. Barundi, Burundi; di Nola, pp. 16 f.

6. Shilluk, Sudan; Mbiti, p. 203. Nyikang is the national founder. In mythology surrounding him he is referred to as son of God, associated with God, and so on. Sacrifices are made to him, and prayers are made to or through him, so that he takes the position of a national intermediary between people and God.

7. Hottentots, South Africa; Quatrefages, p. 209.

8. —?—, South Africa; di Nola, p. 11.

9. Kikuyu, Kenya; Gatheru, p. 4. This prayer is supposed to have been made by the first ancestor of the Kikuyu people (from whom the name is derived).

10. Kipsigis, Kenya; Peristiany, p. 36.

11. Maasai, Kenya and Tanzania; Bleeker, p. 49.

12. Akamba, Kenya; Mbiti, p. 195.

13. Didinga, Sudan; Driberg, p. 97. A black bull (resembling the storm clouds) is sacrificed, and sacred water is sprinkled around. Then the people sing and dance to mark the event of the rain season.

CHAPTER 13

1. Dinka, Sudan; Lienhardt, p. 295.
2. Baronga, Mozambique; di Nola, p. 39.
3. Suk, Kenya; Beech, p. 18.
4. Meru, Tanzania; Harjula, p. 26. Izuva and Murungu are two names of God.
5. Tharaka, Kenya; Bernardi, pp. 121 f.
6. Tharaka, Kenya; Bernardi, p. 112.
7. Meru, Kenya; Bernardi, p. 117.
8. Ngombe, Zaire; J. Davidson in Smith, p. 173. Kunda is the founder of many of the Ngombe clans; *mokanga* is a word of agreement.
9. Ngombe, Zaire; J. Davidson, ibid. A man going on a journey recites this prayer before daybreak, on three consecutive mornings. While reciting it he burns a piece of gum near the sacrificial tree (altar). Having finished naming the animals he has killed, he assembles his family and, taking their hands, spits gently on them to bless them, while chanting the last part of the prayer. This prayer is from a matriarchal clan. Kunda is the founder of many clans.
10. Meru, Kenya; Bernardi, p. 197. When families are not prospering, they visit the *Mugwe* (tribal religious leader) who gives them hospitality in his compound, if they come from afar. The next morning he blesses them, using this prayer.
11. —?—, South Africa; Brown, p. 155. This prayer song is used by the priest-medicineman, when he is waving an offering over the house, lands or villages.
12. Ngombe, Zaire; J. Davidson in Smith, p. 174. Formerly the Ngombe chief would gather his warriors round the sacrificial tree (*libaka*), spit on a smooth stone and mix red camwood powder with the spittle. Then he would rub the red mixture on the forehead of each warrior and, using this prayer, call upon God to help them. At the end of the prayer they would shout their agreement, *mokanga*. Kunda is the ancestor of many Ngombe clans.
13. Ngombe, Zaire; J. Davidson in Smith, pp. 173 f. This prayer is said by a chief on behalf of his people who assemble at the sacrificial tree (*libaka*) early in the morning on his summons, if things are not going well. The blessing is seen in terms of removing the curse which, supposedly, is causing things to go wrong. Kunda is father of many clans. Bilikonda is one of the praise names of God and means 'the unendingness of the forest', i.e. the eternal, the everlasting God.
14. Banyoro, Uganda; Roscoe, p. 111.
15. Meru, Kenya; Bernardi, p. 114.
16. Ga, Ghana; Shorter, p. 11.
17. (a) Banyarwanda, Rwanda; (b) and (c) Mende, Sierra Leone; (d) Nandi, Kenya; (e) Shilluk, Sudan; (f) and (g) Vugusu, Kenya; Mbiti, pp. 207 ff.
18. (a) Akamba, Kenya; (b) Tswana, Botswana; (c) Banyarwanda and Burundi, Rwanda and Burundi; (d) Akamba, Kenya; (e) Banyarwanda and Barundi, Rwanda and Burundi; (f) and (g) Mende, Sierra Leone; (h) Banyarwanda

and Barundi, Rwanda and Burundi; (i) and (j) Tswana, Botswana; (k) Banyarwanda and Barundi, Rwanda and Burundi; Mbiti, pp. 207 ff.

19. (a) Ingassana, Ethiopia; (b) Mende, Sierra Leone; Mbiti, pp. 207 ff.
20. (a) Mende, Sierra Leone; (b) Akamba, Kenya; Mbiti, pp. 207 ff.
21. Wapokomo, Kenya; di Nola, p. 10.
22. Kikuyu, Kenya; di Nola, p. 37.
23. Kikuyu, Kenya; Gatheru, p. 6. This litany is recited while people are proceeding from the sacred tree to the villages.
24. Ga, Ghana; Shorter, p. 10.
25. Ewe, Dahomey, Ghana and Togo; di Nola, p. 41.

Bibliographical sources
of the prayers

Bamunoba, Y. K., personal communication, 1970.

Beech, M. W. H., *The Suk, Their Language and Folklore*, Oxford 1911.

Bleeker, S., *The Masai, Herders of East Africa*, Wm. Morrow and Co., New York 1963.

Brown, J. T., *Among the Bantu Nomads*, Seeley, Service and Co., London 1926.

Busia, K. A., *The Position of the Chief in the Modern Political System of Ashanti*, Oxford University Press, London 1951.

Butt-Thompson, F. W., *West African Secret Societies*, H. F. and G. Witherby, London 1929.

Campbell, D., *In the Heart of Bantu Land*, Seeley, Service and Co., London 1922.

di Nola, A. M., ed., *The Prayers of Man*, William Heinemann, London 1962.

Douglas, M., and Kaberry, P. M., eds., *Man in Africa*, Tavistock London 1969.

Driberg, J. H., I: *The Lango, a Nilotic Tribe of Uganda*, Unwin, London 1923; II: *People of the Small Arrow*, Routledge, London 1930.

East, R., *Akiga's Story*, Oxford University Press, London 1939.

Evans-Pritchard, E. E., I: *Witchcraft, Oracles and Magic among the Azande*, The Clarendon Press, Oxford 1937; II: *Nuer Religion*, The Clarendon Press, Oxford 1956.

Field, J. M., I: *Religion and Medicine of the Ga People*, The Clarendon Press, Oxford 1937; II: *Akim-Kotoku, an Oman of the Gold Coast*, The Crown Agents for Colonies, London 1948.

Gatheru, G. M., *Child of Two Worlds*, Routledge, London 1964.

Griaule, M., *Conversations with Ogotemmeli: an Introduction to Dogon Religious Ideas*, Oxford University Press, London 1965.

Harjula, R., *God and the Sun in Meru Thought*, The Finnish Society for Missiology and Ecumenics, Helsinki 1969.

Hayley, T. T. S., *The Anatomy of Lango Religion*, Cambridge University Press, Cambridge 1947.

Herskovits, M. J., *Dahomey*, Vol. I, J. J. Augustin Publishers, New York 1938.

Hollis, A. C., I: *The Masai*, The Clarendon Press, Oxford 1905;
    II: *The Nandi*, The Clarendon Press, Oxford 1909.

Hudson, D., *Karimojong Politics*, Oxford 1966.

Hunter (Wilson), M., *Reaction to Conquest*, Oxford University Press,
    London 1936.

Idowu, E. B., *Olodumare: God in Yoruba Belief*, Longmans, London
    1962.

Kasenene, P., 'Beliefs, Rituals and Taboos surrounding Beer-trough
    Making among the Banyankore', Occasional Research Paper No. 122,
    Department of Religious Studies and Philosophy, Makerere University,
    Kampala, 1973.

Lienhardt, G., *Divinity and Experience, the Religion of the Dinka*, The
    Clarendon Press, Oxford 1961.

Mbiti, J. S., *Concepts of God in Africa*, S.P.C.K., London and Praeger,
    New York 1970.

Mbotana, J. L., 'Funeral rites and ceremonies of remembering the
    Departed among the Basoga', Occasional Research Paper No. 148,
    Department of Religious Studies and Philosophy, Makerere University,
    Kampala 1973.

Melland, F. H., *In Witchbound Africa*, Seeley, Service and Co., London
    1923.

Merritt, H., draft thesis on Abaluyia Ritual, University of Nairobi 1974.

Ndeti, K., *Elements of Akamba Life*, East Africa Publishing House,
    Nairobi 1972.

Owere, P., 'Bura the Adhola God, before and after the Coming of the
    Catholic Church to Padhola', Occasional Research Paper No. 168,
    Department of Religious Studies and Philosophy, Makerere University,
    Kampala 1973.

Owor, J. S., '*Lamiro gi Chowirok* (Religious Beliefs and Practices)',
    Occasional Research Paper No. 58, Department of Religious Studies
    and Philosophy, Makerere University, Kampala 1972.

Peristiany, J. G., *The Social Institutions of the Kipsigis*, Routledge, London
    1939.

Quatrefages, A. De, *Religion of the Hottentots and Bushmen*, Macmillan,
    London and New York 1895.

Rattray, R. S., *Religion and Art in Ashanti*, Oxford University Press,
    London 1927.

Read, M., *The Ngoni of Nyasaland*, The Clarendon Press, Oxford 1956.

Roscoe, J., *The Bakitara or Banyoro*, Cambridge University Press,
    Cambridge 1923.

Routledge, W. S. and K., *With a Prehistoric People*, Frank Cass, London
    1910.

Russell, J. K., *Men without God?*, The Highway Press, London 1966.

Seligman, C. G., and B. Z., *Pagan Tribes of the Nilotic Sudan*, Routledge, London 1932.

Shorter, A., collector, *The Word That Lives*, Pastoral Institute, Kampala, n.d. (1971).

Smith, E. W. and Dale, A. M., *The Ila Speaking Peoples of Northern Rhodesia*, Vol. I, Macmillan, London 1920.

Wagner, G., *The Bantu of Northern Kavirondo*, Vol. II, Oxford University Press, London 1956.

Index of Prayer Titles

(The number of the prayer in the text is in brackets)

Index of Subjects